The Reasonable Art of Fly Fishing

The Reasonable Art of Fly Fishing

TERRY MORT

Foreword by Tom Rosenbauer

Illustrations by Larry Largay

ABENAKI PUBLISHERS, INC.
Bennington, Vermont

Distributed by The Lyons Press
New York, New York

Printed in the United States of America

Designed by Carol Jessop, Black Trout Design, Shaftsbury, Vermont.

10 9 8 7 6 5 4 3 2 1

Library of Congress Cataloging-in-Publication Data
Mort, Terry
The reasonable art of fly fishing / Terry Mort
ISBN 1-55821-683-9
1. Fly fishing—Instruction   2. Mort, Terry   I. Title

The publishers have generously given permission to use quotations from the following copyrighted works. From *A River Runs Through It*, by Norman Maclean. Copyright 1976 by the University of Chicago. Reprinted by permission of the publisher, The University of Chicago Press. Excerpt from *By-Line: Ernest Hemingway*, "Fishing the Rhone Canal," by Ernest · Hemingway. Excerpted with permission of Scribner, a Division of Simon & Schuster, from *By-Line: Ernest Hemingway*, edited by William White. Originally appeared in the Toronto Daily Star. Copyright © 1967 by Mary Hemingway. Excerpt from *Patterns of Culture* by Ruth Benedict. Copyright © 1934 by Ruth Benedict, © renewed 1961 by Ruth Valentine. Reprinted by permission of Houghton Mifflin Co. All rights reserved. From *Picasso*, by Patrick O'Brian. Copyright © 1976 by Patrick O'Brian. Reprinted by permission of Georges Borchardt, Inc. for the author.

o Colin,

my son

and fishing buddy

Contents

oreword

FRIEND OF MINE RECENTLY MADE AN OFFHAND STATEMENT that was so patently obvious but so profound that it made a big impression on me: "Most of us came to fly fishing through reading." All the people I know who are dedicated, sicko, passionate fly fishers are also serious readers, and those I have asked admit to having read about fly fishing before they had ever cast a fly. I don't think you can make the same statement about hunting or golf or bicycling. I'm sorry I didn't have a copy of Terry Mort's book thirty years ago.

The finest line fly-fishing writers tread is that between literature and exposition. Some of them strive for useful, clear prose that best transmits information to a novice, knowing it will never be considered fine literature. Some attempt to capture the essence of fly fishing in prose, a nearly insurmountable task that usually ends up quite purple. Tom McGuane and Craig Nova and Nick Lyons come closest to the real thing. A very few achieve a level of communication that passes on valuable knowledge while entertaining in an intimate way that seems to place the writer at the elbow of the reader. John Atherton's 1953 book *The Fly and the Fish* was successful in this way, at least for me when I was twelve years old. Sparse Grey Hackle could do it. So can John Gierach. And now Terry Mort joins this select group, with a literate introduction to fly fishing, the most readable and fun introduction I have ever read.

Terry has been around this fly-fishing business a long time. More than fifteen years ago, before most households even had VCR machines, he came to me with an idea to produce a fly-tying video. He insisted the video be honest and accurate, without a lot of scripting, yet filmed by an Emmy-award-winning cameraman. Terry and I became good friends during this project, and I had the pleasure of guiding Terry's son, Colin, to his first trout on a fly. I still treasure the picture of little Colin (now graduated from college and about a foot taller than I am) proudly hoisting a tiny wild rainbow, adult-size sunglasses perched precariously on his nose and occupying about three-quarters of his face. Terry's day job is running seminars for high-level executives around the world, and I wish I had an excuse to attend one, if this book is any example of his teaching technique.

If I were asked to teach someone to fish with a fly I would require that he read this book first. There is no substitute for being taught by a patient mentor, followed by lots of time in the field, making your own mistakes, immersing yourself in a local trout stream or bass pond. But the overwhelming temptation in these days of limited time is to read about fly fishing when you can't do it, especially when you are starting out and can't get enough of this satisfying pastime. Unfortunately, the stuff you read in magazines and books these days is often dry, pretentiously pseudoscientific, and filled with jargon. Terry's book is different. When I agreed to write the foreword I had imagined he had written a collection of amusing essays of his fishing around the world, from Ireland to Idaho, but as I got into Terry's manuscript I discovered a literate, sensible, and readable introduction to fly fishing. No other introduction to fly fishing quotes Shakespeare, George Bernard Shaw, and Mark Twain, among many others, and makes them fit perfectly into the discourse.

What will *The Reasonable Art of Fly Fishing* do for you? It will provide you with a glossary for all that silly jargon we fly fishers use, but the teaching will creep up on you and you won't realize you're being taught. Catch-and-release fishing is often seen as a Siamese twin of fly fishing, but Terry Mort helps you make your own decision and lets you develop your own ethic on catch-and-release and other aspects of the sport that introductory texts often omit. Yet he doesn't preach; again, you'll be encouraged to make up your own mind. Above all, Terry's goal is to make sure each reader gets what he or she wants out of fly fishing.

One of the acid tests of an introductory book about a skill that requires hand-eye coordination is that the text allow the reader to learn a skill independent of the illustrations, the graphics being just a reinforcement of the text. Fly casting is very difficult to teach in person, and even more so in print, yet this book contains the best, the most interesting, and the most effective introduction to fly casting I have ever read. And when I wrote this foreword I had not yet seen the illustrations, just the manuscript.

I think Terry puts the emphasis in the right places, but perhaps that's my own bias. I have seen many would-be fly fishers intimidated by mayflies before they had even seen one, reasoning by what they had read that unless they could follow a binomial key in *Usinger's Aquatic Insects of California* they would not be able to convince a cold-blooded critter with a brain the size of a pea to strike a fake fly. Terry puts us on the right track. He doesn't neglect entomology, but he devotes twice as many words to trout behavior, a far more interesting and useful pastime if you must introduce a scientific bent into your fishing. If we were more interested in bugs than fish we'd be running around with butterfly nets and jars of formaldehyde.

If this is your first fly-fishing book, you are very fortunate—you're starting off on the right track. If you've read others before, I think you'll agree with me that you wish this had been your first.

Tom Rosenbauer
Manchester, Vermont

Preface

THERE ARE MANY BEAUTIFULLY WRITTEN, INFORMATIVE BOOKS on fishing, particularly fly fishing. Some are even minor works of art. No other sport has generated so much literary effort. Angling literature consists of reminiscences, technical information, how-to and where-to manuals, travel stories, natural history and biology, entomology, river and stream descriptions, and assorted other musings. Angling references also bob up frequently in poetry and fiction. Shakespeare, John Donne, W. B. Yeats, Ernest Hemingway—to name just four—used angling as both metaphor and context. (Opinion among the scribbling class is not unanimously positive. I think it was Oscar Wilde who described angling as a fish at one end of a line and a fool at the other. But Wilde was rarely mistaken for an outdoorsman, and we may safely dismiss his witticism as the product of ignorance, a joke for joking's sake.)

Something about fly fishing seems to stimulate the literary glands. Why is this? Partly, it has to do with the setting—sometimes awesomely beautiful, sometimes calm and peaceful, sometimes wild and in a way intimidating. The environment of gamefish, particularly of trout, is invariably interesting and attractive. People who like to talk, talk about it; people who like to paint, paint it; people who like to write, write about it. These urges are a force of nature. You might as well try to plug Niagara or keep a fat boy from dessert. It's as though the fly attracts both the trout and the angler who casts it. The one rises to what seems to be food, the other to what seems to be truth. Or at least, meaning. And, having perceived a glimmer of meaning, people try to get it down on paper.

Then there's the mystery of it all. Why do these creatures, especially trout, do what they do? Despite our understanding of their biology and their basic behavior, they still baffle us now and then, and this enjoyable frustration gives rise to literary pondering—"If there were world enough and time, this coyness, Salmo, were no crime."

Then too there are the pleasant memories that angling creates. If we can believe Wordsworth when he says that poetry is strong emotion recollected in tranquillity, then something very like poetry resides in the hearts of all anglers, who spend many a winter's afternoon thinking back on a summer's day when the fish were rising and the weather was cooperating and God was indeed in His Heaven and all was right with the world, for once. People who have a literary bent naturally want to express these pleasurable feelings and thereby recreate the time and hold it fast. They also want to share it with other initiates. And some want to baptize the heathen. There are few greater satisfactions than introducing someone to something that you know will provide a lifetime of pleasure. It is like giving a friend his first collection of P. G. Wodehouse stories.

So, people like to write about fishing, and a great many have done it. Considering all the words that have been expended on the subject of angling, you might wonder why anyone would do another book on the subject. What can possibly be the point? What is there left to say? These are questions I asked myself. I'm not sure I came up with a very satisfactory answer. But here it is, such as it is:

First, there's the question of context. Many of the fly-fishing books I have seen concentrate on technique or equipment. There's nothing wrong with that, but a new book on the old subject did not seem worth doing. It occurred to me, though, that some of these books overlook the fact that technique is a means to an end, rather than an end in itself. Casting books will tell you how to get the fly in the right place. *Why* that place is right is implied. In this book I try to show that fly fishing is a reasonable art; that is, a reasonable response to the interrelated factors of flowing water, aquatic food sources, and trout behavior, that all three are inextricably intertwined and from their interrelationship flow all of the considerations of form, technique, and equipment. I try to make the "why" of fly fishing explicit so that the "how" seems more reasonable.

Second, a lot of angling books and articles tend to overwhelm you with information. But all information is not of equal value; some ideas are fundamental, others are peripheral, still others merely decorative. If you were going to explain ethics to a Martian, for example, you could start by having him read the complete works of Spinoza and then report back, or you could give him a copy of the Ten Commandments and build from there. There's nothing wrong with Spinoza, but he's a little more than anyone needs at the start. Similarly, if you want to learn about fly fishing you could read a book on entomology followed by books on rod construction and casting technique. You'd get through it all eventually, but it would take a little time. Since the primary object of fly fishing is enjoyment, why not learn the fundamentals and then have at it? You'll pick up more as you go along. (It is literally true that I have never had a day of fishing when I didn't learn something.) In this book I try to focus on the essentials and let the other nice-to-know information go for another time.

The mere fact that a book is published does not prove that the author can write or that he knows what he is talking about. It only proves that he was able to convince a publisher to print it. Fortunately for angling authors, fly fishing is one of those complex arts that has few rights and wrongs, few immutable laws. As in a democracy, everyone is welcome to an opinion, sometimes several, and he is welcome to publish those opinions, if he can find an accomplice. Therefore, even the occasional author who turns out unreadable stuff better suited to wrapping fish than describing them rarely does any real damage. Fly fishing is just a sport, after all, and it can accommodate a wide range of differing views. I confess that a lot of what follows is just opinion—mine and those of people I respect. Whether these opinions and ideas are well informed and expressed is, of course, for you to decide. But your heart is obviously in the right place, for you have a fly-fishing book in your hands. Can a stream be far away?

A *Reasonable* Art

No man is born an artist, so no man is born an angler.
   —Izaak Walton, *The Compleat Angler*

From the moment of his birth the customs into which [an individual] is born shape his experience and behavior .... he is a little creature of his culture.
   —Ruth Fulton Benedict, *Patterns of Culture*

I DON'T SUPPOSE TROUT HAVE A "CULTURE" in the usual sense of the word, though there's no way to tell for sure, since there's a lot about trout that humans don't know. But certainly the idea that creatures are products of their surroundings applies to fish as well as to humans.

Viewed in that light, the things a trout does are reasonable, even logical. The trout's behavior is the result of the conditions in which he finds himself. In other words, his behavior stems from basic needs: a dependable supply of food, safety from predators, and an environment that won't asphyxiate, poison, or wear him out. Every now and then a trout feels the urge to procreate, and for that he needs a partner and, if not privacy, at least congenial surroundings. That pretty much covers everything trout need. Their requirements are simple and unvarying, and generally dictate the way they behave.

Those of us who want to catch trout need to understand these conditions and the behavior that derives from them. This doesn't mean we all have to be ichthyologists or ecologists or entomologists or anything of that sort. It just means that if we understand why a trout behaves the way he does, we have a better chance of fooling the trout into thinking our scraps of feathers and fur are

something he normally eats. Understanding the trout's behavior also allows us to enter into his world without disturbing it, and allows us to synchronize ourselves to the trout's invariably interesting environment; and that is both a means to an end (catching fish) and an end in itself (knowledge that is satisfying and enriching for its own sake).

The essence of fly fishing is deception. Perhaps that's why it appeals to so many people. It's a benign sort of trickery. As Shakespeare says in *Much Ado About Nothing*:

> Sigh no more, ladies, sigh no more.
> Men were deceivers ever;
> One foot in the sea, and one on shore;
> To one thing constant never.

Perhaps, when Shakespeare talks about never being constant to one thing, he is referring to our habit of changing flies promiscuously. But certainly we anglers are deceivers. Fortunately for the trout, most of the time we're happy enough with a successful deception, and we don't need to keep the trout after his gullibility has served our purpose. (Speaking of Shakespeare, it may be interesting to remember that in the same play he says: "Bait the hook well: this fish will bite." This reference to bait fishing has disappointed many people who otherwise would have thought well of the Bard.)

So we study the trout's behavior and environment in order to trick him into biting. We know that the trout's behavior is reasonable, given his needs; and by understanding those needs and creating the kinds of situations that simulate reality, we can deceive him and bring him to the net. That's the more-or-less reasonable part of fly fishing. So far, so good.

Yes, but is it art? Maybe. Consider the following:

First, it's an art because it is not a science. There are no formulas for success. Anglers venturing off in the morning wish each other good luck for a reason. Regardless of how accomplished a deceiver one becomes, sometimes the trout win. Sometimes they ignore our beseeching, like coy mistresses, equally infuriating and dispiriting. They recognize our blandishments for the false promises they are, and we splash toward the bank at the end of the day, beaten. By a fish! And, worse yet, sometimes we are at a loss to explain how or why it happened. This is part of the art of the business—the mystery of it all. If it were all science, we would never be skunked. We would apply the appropriate formula and—*Voila*! But it is an art, because it not only calls for technique but also allows for intuition and hunches and creativity and surprises and luck. This is not to say that science cannot play a part. Some anglers know all the Latin names of the aquatic insects that trout eat, and they know the biology of the trout and all the other creatures in the stream. But even those erudite anglers get shut out sometimes. There is very little of the scientific method in fly fishing; there is no set process that you can apply in order to create predictable results.

Then, too, fly fishing is an art because it does have a reasonably set structure, a beginning, middle, and end. In the first act, the angler arrives on the scene and studies the situation. He looks at the stream for likely places where trout should be or notices the rings on the surface that indicate a feeding trout. The second act involves figuring out what the trout is eating, selecting a fly that resembles the natural food, and determining a strategy for getting the fly to the fish in a way that deceives him. In the third act, the angler casts the fly—presents it to the fish—and, if all goes according to plan, the fish accepts it and, after a struggle, comes reluctantly to the net. When all three acts come together perfectly, the successful angler feels a pleasure that is all out of proportion to the tangible result, a fish. This pleasure is related in part to the satisfaction of participating in an aesthetically well-constructed event. A sense of completeness and closure is present in most good art, and absent in most other kinds of experience. Non-anglers who are mystified about why catching such a small and biologically unsophisticated creature can create so much pleasure miss the point that the enjoyment comes not so much from the substance of the event—the acquisition of a fish—but from the form, from the drama in which the angler is not only the actor but also the director and playwright. And the pleasure comes not only from the event itself, but also from the recollection of the event, as in any good art.

Here's another artistic aspect to consider: fly fishing incorporates techniques similar to those used in painting. In one sense, fly fishing is like *trompe l'oeil* painting, the astonishingly realistic technique that literally fools the eye into thinking the picture is real. After all, that's what we are trying to do to the fish: trick him into thinking that what he is seeing is real. On the other hand, fly fishing is not unlike impressionist painting, since the flies we use are rarely precise copies of the real thing. Instead, trout flies are more like impressions, approximations of the real. They suggest to the trout that they are edible. And, to stretch the analogy to the breaking point, many trout flies don't imitate anything in nature— they are just abstractions invented by anglers who know that trout will sometimes strike at flies simply out of aggression or curiosity. (Salmon flies, for example, are all abstractions, since salmon don't feed when they are coming upstream to spawn. Why they strike at these flies is a subject of much debate and no certainty.)

So, as you see, there are many parallels between fly fishing and painting, but the common denominator in all of this is the attempt to attract or deceive the eye, either of the art lover or the trout.

But…"Oh what a tangled web we [sometimes] weave, When first we practice to deceive."

Anyone who has thrown a fly line into the wind—or into the trees along the bank—knows just how tangled things can get. It's not easy to fool Mother Nature, and it's not easy to fool a trout, either, at least not with a fly rod. Therein lies another aspect of the art of fly fishing. No one picks up a fly rod for the first time and starts catching fish. It takes a little practice. A little craftsmanship. That's part of the fun. After all, if we just wanted to *acquire* trout, we would net them and be done with it (or use a worm or a cheese-ball). It's the way we catch them that makes it fun. Most of the time we just throw them back, anyway. The art of catching them is the reason we do this. The process is the goal. The means is the end. Doing it is the point. It is art for art's sake. The trout is not really the objective; he is a participant in the game, and playing the game is the goal. It is more a matter of form than content.

Then there are the restrictions of the medium. Any art is limited by the nature of the materials. A painter can't create something that is truly three-dimensional. The medium won't allow it. Similarly, the rules and restrictions of nature, of the stream and the behavior of its denizens, restrict what the angler can do—he must understand and conform to these restrictions or he will fail.

Finally, fly fishing is an art because it helps us to see more clearly. It helps us see by requiring us to look at things in a different way—to look at a stream not as a ribbon of water next to an interstate highway, but rather as a three-dimensional…what? Organism? System? Those words are too clinical. Something alive? That's closer to it. The point here is that angling requires us to look more thoroughly than we would otherwise look. And in so doing we can't help but *see* more than we otherwise would. Izaak Walton's famous dictum, "Study to be quiet," applies here, and the emphasis is on "study," as in "look carefully and think about what you see." (We will skip over the fact that Walton, too, was a bait fisherman. His heart was in the right place.) Once hooked on the sport, a fly fisherman will never again be able to drive across a bridge without looking at the stream below. Fly fishing allows us to see things that we used to miss.

But let's not step too far into the deep end. If there's a hole that many people fall into when discussing or writing about fly fishing, it's getting rhapsodic. (*Mea culpa.*) Prose tends to get a little purple around the edges; descriptions tend to get a little poetic; explanations tend to get intellectualized. We'll try to resist these siren calls from here on. The point is that fly fishing is a reasonable art because trout behavior is—if not predictable—at least explicable. Usually. And if you understand their environment and the ways they have adapted their behavior to it, and if you develop and refine your technique, you can catch some of them, some of the time. And doing it is serious fun and seriously satisfying, like any good art.

And more good news—anyone can do this, anyone can be an artist. You don't have to use fancy equipment or materials to be effective and have fun doing it. You don't have to be born with any particular talent; you just have to be willing to practice and learn. There's an endless amount of information to acquire. No one knows everything about fly fishing for trout—no one. The limits of different people's knowledge are just different, that's all. So no one need be intimidated by fly fishing, because not even the professionals (and there are people who earn their living from fly fishing) have all the answers. The more one knows, the more one realizes how much is left to learn. That cliché is particularly true about fly fishing. (An aquatic insect was found on the Snake River in Idaho last year that no one had ever seen before and that an entomologist could not identify, yet it was food for trout, presumably, and therefore an element in the art of fly fishing.) So you can be whatever kind of angling artist you want to be—a Michelangelo or a finger-painter, a serious student or a dabbler. Every person's idea of angling pleasure is different, and fly fishing can accommodate them all. The trout don't care. While you're having fun, they're just trying to make a living.

Water

All Gaul is divided into three parts.
—Julius Caesar, *De Bello Gallico*

LIKE CAESAR, THE FLY FISHERMAN SURVEYS HIS DOMAIN and sees that it has three parts. Those parts are moving water, food, and the trout. The three elements are inextricably joined together into a natural process, like three strands in a braid. In fact, the fly fisherman's domain is a process, not a place— a constantly changing scene made up of these elements which, themselves, are constantly changing. Disturb one of the elements and the process is interrupted, perhaps halted. Humans are interlopers in that process. We are there to fish for trout, but if we are going to be successful we need to understand and adapt to the natural processes, understand each element and how that element interacts with the other two. And the first of these elements is water.

MOVING WATER

The favorite philosopher of all right-thinking anglers is Heraclitus, for it was he who said: "You could not step twice into the same rivers; for other waters are ever flowing on to you." In other words, the essence of a river is change, movement. Current. (Heraclitus also said "It is better to hide ignorance, but it is hard to do when we relax over wine"—one more reason why he should be the fly fisherman's patron philosopher.)

It's obvious that trout do not always live in rivers and streams. Some trout live quite happily in lakes. Some even migrate to the oceans, where they spend several years before they return to fresh water to spawn. But for our purposes, we need to think about fly fishing for trout in rivers and in streams—in moving water.

Consider this: You are standing on a bridge spanning a small stream, and in your hand you have a bag of cheese puffs. You drop one of the cheese puffs into the stream. What happens next? The cheese puff is swept away by the current. It doesn't travel in a straight line, because there are swirls and eddies and maybe rocks, which divert the current and change the course of the cheese puff. Also, there are probably several different currents in the stream, each with a different course and speed. But regardless of the unique characteristics of this stream, the key is that the cheese puff travels downstream, borne by the current until, perhaps, it disappears suddenly in a splashy riseform made by a fish with a taste for snack food. A trout.

Next, you drop another cheese puff in the same place and watch as it travels, and you notice that it ends up downstream in pretty much the same place and probably suffers the same fate. Now suppose that while you are musing on the bridge, the wind comes up and blows a grasshopper off the grassy bank near the bridge into the water below you. While the grasshopper might not have landed exactly where you had earlier dropped the cheese puff, it is swept into the same current line, travels roughly the same course, and ultimately ends up at the same place—in the belly of a fish with a taste for grasshoppers, too.

What is the meaning of this experiment ?

It means that the current can—and generally does—deliver food to predictable places as it constantly moves along the stream bed. Current is reliable. The only time this changes is when the stream's normal patterns are disrupted by drought or flood or release of water from a dam upstream, or by rocks or trees that fall into the stream and alter the current's direction. But, all things being constant in terms of the amount of water flow, the current will deliver food to a fish in a predictable pattern. (We'll discuss where the food comes from later on. Assume for now that Nature is dropping the cheese puffs.) The stream is like an endless assembly line, and the trout are the workers poised all along the line. A trout can depend on the current and can, therefore, be territorial—he can find a spot where the current delivers reliable supplies of food and just stay there. This is a primary difference between trout that live in streams and trout that live in lakes. In a lake, there is no constant surface current (although there are intermittent currents caused by wind, and there may be subsurface springs which cause currents), and the trout therefore has to cruise the lake in search of food. In a stream, the trout lets the current bring the food to him.

This is not to say that everything is beer and skittles for trout in rivers and streams. They have to struggle against the current to maintain their positions, and so they must find places that don't require too much effort to hold. If the current is too strong, trout use up more energy fighting to hold in one spot than they can take in from their conveyor belt of food. Trout are constantly calculating the cost/benefit ratio. Their cost is the energy they expend to acquire food; the benefit is the energy they receive from the food. When the cost exceeds the benefit (because the current is too swift or the delivery of food too scanty), they must find another place or face starvation.

At the risk of stating the obvious, trout that live in rivers and streams and depend on the current to deliver food face upstream, their noses into the current. That way they can see the food as it drifts down to them. Trout will not notice food that lands behind them, such as a grasshopper that drops off the bank just downstream. The trout's attention is directed upstream. And of course, he is admirably streamlined for his profession. Compare his sleek lines to the shape of, say, a largemouth bass, and the difference is roughly the same as the difference between a Formula One racer and a Volvo. Furthermore, the reason a trout is slippery is that it is covered with a layer of slime that helps it to slide through the water.

A trout in a stream or river is territorial. Further, there is no sense of sportsmanship or chivalry among trout. They are all business. The biggest and the meanest fish take and keep the best holding spots, or "lies." The smaller guys have to take second best, or worse. (They also have to watch out for their larger cousins, who are just as happy to eat trout as cheese puffs, maybe more so. It's always something when you're the low one on the totem pole.)

Being territorial does not mean that trout find a spot and then stay there from adolescence through retirement. They will move around, especially if the stream's characteristics change drastically for one reason or another (floods, dams, man-made changes, natural erosion or sculpting of the streambed, and so on). And, of course, as a trout grows, he needs more food and therefore a better lie, and he has more clout when he wants to evict smaller fish from desirable positions. But as a general rule, the trout is looking to find a reliable and comfortable place to intercept current-borne food, and when he finds such a place, he tends to stay there. When it comes to selecting a place to live, trout may not be buyers, but they definitely tend to prefer long-term leases.

Another important observation from our cheese-puff experiment is that the current is in control. The food is trapped; it must quite literally go with the flow. Most of the food that trout take from the surface is in the same predicament—generally it cannot escape from the current, either because it can't swim well or because it's half drowned and therefore too depressed to try, or because the current's just too strong or it's caught in the invisible film called surface tension. Whatever the reason, the food moves in and with the current— same speed, same direction. If the current swerves, the food swerves. If it is straight, the course of the food is straight. This food, as we will see in greater detail later, is primarily insects. These insects come in two categories—aquatic insects which live in the stream and terrestrial insects which live on land but for a variety of reasons (wind, bad luck, miscalculation) find themselves afloat.

So here's the point—the food is caught in the current, and the current moves in a predictable direction and speed that the trout has come to understand and depend on. The trout is waiting and watching. He expects this waterborne food to behave in a certain way, trapped as it is in the current. Therefore, anything that does not match this motion, this expected speed and direction, will appear unnatural to the trout, and he will most likely avoid it. To the trout, any morsel not floating normally could not be food—it is not behaving as food behaves, since food behaves the way the current dictates. The obvious implication for the fly fisherman is that unless he can make his lure—his fly—duplicate the natural motion of current-borne food, his offering will immediately be perceived to be unnatural (even frightening) by the trout and most likely will be avoided. A key principle of fly fishing, therefore, is that we have to be able to *match the motion* of the natural food. *How* we do that is something we'll get to later. *That* we must do it is a function of the natural process, the trout's relationship with—and understanding of—the current. To put it another way, deception lies in the motion, the behavior of the lure.

Here's another rule of thumb: All of these principles are just generalizations, and trout will occasionally do something that contradicts them. (As someone once said, all generalizations are false, including this one.) For example, now and then a trout will chase an angler's fly that is dragging across the current or, even more bizarrely, floating against the current and therefore acting like nothing in nature, nothing the trout has ever seen before. (I once was trudging upstream with my rod over my shoulder and the fly dragging in the water 20 feet behind me, and I suddenly felt a tug and turned around to see a very large cutthroat trout thrashing around at the end of my line.) Why trout should occasionally do something stupid is inexplicable. But they do. Maybe they're curious or aggressive or cantankerous that day. But the important point is that they don't do that sort of thing very often. Anglers who depend on trout to be stupid should have a high tolerance for disappointment.

The foregoing applies to food that is on the surface of the stream—things such as grasshoppers and other insects that float downstream in the current. Trout do eat other stuff, including their smaller brethren. And it's obvious that minnows and small fry do not float on the surface, but rather dart around beneath the surface trying to snare a morsel now and then while at the same time staying off someone else's menu. This food source is not directly affected or borne by the current. Still, the principle of matching the natural motion applies to food that lives below the surface, too, as we will see later on. What's more, current is not just a surface phenomenon; it is three-dimensional, and so affects everything living in the stream. Further, the strength of the current varies according to the depth of the water. The general rule is that the velocity of the current is slower nearer the floor of the stream, because of the friction of the water against the streambed. The trout can therefore lie low in a pool and conserve energy while looking up to see food that floats by as well as straight ahead at the food tumbling along the streambed.

To say that trout are territorial is not to say that they are stationary. Often a trout will have two positions, two lies. The first is his holding lie, the place where he prefers to hang out when resting. Generally, in this position the trout will not be eating, although he will not pass up a morsel that floats conveniently past his nose. The primary criteria for selecting a holding lie are safety from predators and energy conservation. A holding lie therefore will often be a deep pool which protects the trout from most predators. It will also be away from the strongest currents, since energy must be spent to hold a position against the current, and a trout in a holding lie will want to spend as little energy as possible while resting. His other position is his feeding lie. When the trout decides it's time to eat, he will move to this position, which will be close to a reliable current, meaning a current line that will deliver a reliable supply of food. Sometimes these two positions will be quite close to each other. An undercut bank, for example, is an excellent holding lie because of the protection it affords, and it is also often alongside a current line that delivers food and therefore requires only the smallest movement to snare a drifting insect.

Trout also move around from one lie to another as the season progresses. Studies indicate that some trout will move several miles during the warmer months. Other trout, however, will find a good holding and feeding lie and stay there throughout the season, perhaps throughout their lifetime. Their primary needs—safety, food, and a congenial environment—will dictate the degree to which they wander. The fact that different studies prove different things indicates that no one is really all that sure about trout behavior. It appears to be a matter of different behavior for different streams. Trout behavior, like politics, is mostly local.

During the fall months, most species of trout will spawn. (Some trout—some rainbows and cutthroats—spawn in the spring, but their nesting behavior and environmental requirements are the same as for fall spawners.) For spawning they will need very clear, highly oxygenated moving water and a gravelly bottom in which the female can easily dig out the nests where she will then deposit the eggs. The male hovers alongside and fertilizes the eggs as the female lays them. The water constantly washes over the eggs and is an essential ingredient in their development. Since the riffled, gravel-bottomed water they need is often at the headwaters of a stream, trout that are in the mood to spawn will often travel far upstream to find the perfect spot.

Once spawning is completed in the fall, trout will start to move to their winter quarters, which are usually deep holes in the streambed where they can conserve energy through the long winter months and, if lucky, avoid being crushed by ice. Generally, they don't feed actively during this period, but simply hold until the coming of spring (and with it the arrival of their partners in the great game, the anglers).

Trout might be territorial in the sense that they are not constantly cruising to find dinner, but they are not necessarily always in the same spot. The key concept is that they depend on the current to deliver food, and therefore try to find places that deliver the best, most reliable service. Another way to think about their territoriality is to remember that trout are essentially loners. They don't travel in schools. They have a Garboesque requirement for privacy. This characteristic may in part explain their appeal, since angling tends to be a solitary business. Certainly it is not a team sport, so perhaps there is some psychological affinity or sympathy between fish and fisherman which explains their mutual requirement for remote streams and quiet days.

One final point about territoriality—it also depends to a large extent on the *kind* of stream the trout are living in. Some streams are offer greater incentive to stay in one spot, while others offer rewards for moving around. And that brings us to the subject of streams—and how different streams affect trout behavior.

TYPES OF TROUT STREAMS

For aught that I could ever read,
Could ever hear by tale or history,
The course of true love never did run smooth.
　　　　　　　　　　　　—William Shakespeare,
　　　　　　　　　　　　A Midsummer's Night's Dream

Unlike true love, rivers sometimes do run smooth. Calm. Reasonable. Some rivers, that is. Others are more passionate, unforgiving, boisterous, sometimes shallow, stony-hearted, treacherous, and given to mood swings. It's no wonder we like to be around rivers; they are endlessly interesting.

All rivers and streams have current. All trout who live in rivers and streams rely to a great extent on the current to deliver food to them. But every river or stream has its own characteristics. Streams and rivers fall into two basic categories, depending on the source of their water: runoff streams and spring-fed streams.

Runoff streams are also called "freestone." Fed by melting snows and rainfall that collects in the hills and mountains, these streams rise and fall with changes in weather. They are sometimes swollen and wild, and other times shallow and anemic. People speak of river "drainages," and although that's not a very elegant term, it's a pretty accurate description of the phenomenon. The river valley drains the surrounding countryside of rainwater and snowmelt. Such rivers are also called "spate," which reflects the fact that their volume rises and falls according to the amount of rain and runoff occurring during the year. They are by definition subject to floods and droughts, so the trout will in some periods find themselves avoiding roiling brown spates while at other times they'll be looking for a pool, any pool, because a drought has come and there's not enough water for the trout. The vast majority of streams and rivers in this country are fed by runoff. In alpine areas such as the Rockies, the snowpack is usually so thick that there's a reliable source of runoff, even when there's not much rain in the warmer months. But people in the Western states who are interested in fishing do tend to get a little concerned when the snows are later or lighter than usual.

The other category is the spring-fed streams, sometimes called spring creeks. As the name suggests, these streams do not depend on runoff for their water. They are fed by underground springs, and so the supply of water throughout the year tends to be even, unlike the feast-and-famine cycles of the runoff streams. Further, the temperature of a spring creek tends to be fairly constant throughout the year; it is relatively warm in the winter months (and rarely freezes over) and relatively cool in the summer months. Because of the springs which feed it, the stream's temperature stays within a narrow band throughout the year, and that band is particularly suitable for trout, which prefer fairly cool water; 60 to 65 degrees is pretty much ideal.

The classic spring creek ambles through a grassy meadow and has a calm, almost civilized, demeanor. Its elevation does not drop rapidly; instead, the stream flows almost imperceptibly. The surface of the water is smooth, and an angler has to look carefully to see that the current is in fact moving rather swiftly, is not of uniform speed, and that there are swirls and varying current lines here and there. From a distance, a spring creek looks like an elongated lake. Its water is clear, and its bottom visible. Often the bottom consists of gravel and is characterized by long weeds undulating in the current. Depth is fairly uniform from one bank to the other, and a wading angler is less likely to encounter the deep holes that often surprise him in freestone streams.

If you were a trout and had a choice, you probably would prefer a spring creek—for a number of reasons. First, there would be few if any changes in the flow of the water. The current would be constant and dependable, and you wouldn't need to be looking for a new home because of floods or droughts. In a sense, living in a spring creek is like living on an annuity, while in runoff streams trout are subject to the vagaries of the market. Second, for a variety of reasons (chemical composition, plant life, and a resulting richness of insect and other foods) spring creeks are an easier environment. The current isn't violent. There are numerous hiding places: the weeds that carpet much of the bottom offer refuge while at the same time providing a first-rate habitat for the kinds of food trout like to eat—chiefly insects, small shrimps, and other crustaceans. The temperature of the water is almost constant throughout the year, and for a trout the difference between living in a spring creek and living in a freestone is roughly the same as the difference between living in southern California versus Chicago. At least as far as weather is concerned, the choice is clear. But trout don't have much of a choice. They are where they are.

In a spring creek, there are few if any disturbances on the surface—no protruding rocks or rapids or riffles. (Riffles are essentially mini-rapids: fast water flowing over small stones.) As a result, when trout are feeding on the surface of smooth water, eating food that is floating down to them, their rises are obvious to anyone watching from the bank. They splash or leave rings in the water, depending on how aggressively they're taking food. In any case, you can see them: the surface is so calm that any disturbance is noticeable.

They, in turn, can see you. And they can see your line and leader, and they can see when your cast plops inelegantly, and they can see the bow wave you make as you wade out toward them and the shadow you make and just about everything else. They get a very good look at your fly, and they have time to compare it to the natural things they're eating and to decide whether it looks reasonably natural or whether it's an obvious fraud in either composition or behavior (i.e., motion). So, in smooth-water fishing, you see the whole thing being acted out, and so does the trout.

In a freestone stream, you cannot always see the rises the trout make, because the water is disturbed by riffles and rapids and eddies and so on. You don't always know, therefore, that there is a trout in a particular place. You only know that there should be a trout in certain places, because those places are more logical lies than others. You read the motion of the current and decide where you would go if you were a trout interested in the optimal ratio between expended energy and a regular food supply. And you throw your fly there. Broken water is a little more forgiving than smooth water. The effects of a blacksmith-style cast are masked somewhat by the riffles and dancing currents. Of course, if the fly lands like a depth charge or your line splashes down like a steel reinforcing rod, a trout is likely to notice. Freestone streams are forgiving, but not to the point of being saintly.

In a spring creek, the trout tend to move around when feeding more than they do in a freestone stream. They are less territorial. That may seem strange at first, since the environment is so rich you'd think one spot would be as good as another. Why move? It is because the environment is so rich in food, the weed beds so rife with insects and shrimps, that a trout does not have to depend on one lie, and since there is no violent current to combat, a fish can graze like a goose on a golf course. It's difficult, if not impossible, for an angler to "read the water." It all looks pretty much the same. There are no obvious feeding lies; the trout are feeding anywhere and everywhere. As a result, in fishing spring creeks you generally have to spot a fish that is feeding regularly and throw your fly at him. But while a trout in a spring creek will wander around while feeding, he will also tend to stay in the same general area of the stream. Why move your headquarters when everything you need is right on your doorstep?

Freestone trout move around according to the nature of their particular stream. In streams that have a regular scattering of boulders and rocks sticking up above the surface (called pocket water), trout tend to be very territorial once they find a good spot. The rocks provide a shield against the current; they also direct the water in a predictable fashion and therefore deliver a reliable supply of food. A trout can lie just inside the current line, slightly behind a protruding rock, and shelter himself from the current while in a position to grab anything that floats by. In pocket water, an angler can "read the water"—spot likely lies and drift a fly over them. In all probability, a fish is there, and he might take the fly if it's well presented—that is, if it floats by naturally. Then again, he might not.

Other freestone streams that don't contain pocket water may require the trout to move around in search of good holding and feeding lies as the season progresses and the water levels rise and fall. But in all cases the trout is relying on the current to deliver food, and his main problem will be to find a position that supplies food but doesn't require too much energy to maintain.

Different streams present different problems to the fly fisherman, but in all cases the key thing to remember is that the trout use the current to deliver food, and they expect that food to act naturally as it floats in the current. If the "food" acts in a way contrary to a trout's vast experience with and perception of the current, he will most likely pass up the meal.

There are variations on these categories. Many streams are combinations of the two, fed by both runoff and springs, and some, like the Henrys Fork, have spring-creek characteristics in some places (such as the Railroad Ranch stretch) and freestone characteristics in other places. Then, too, it is possible to create spring-creek conditions—at the base of a dam, for example. The San Juan River in northwestern New Mexico has four miles of spring-creek fishing because the water is released from the Navajo Dam, and the water comes from the deepest and coldest part of the impoundment. As long as the releases of water are fairly regular and the volume fairly constant, the conditions just below the dam match the natural conditions in a spring creek, and the result is four miles of superb fishing. Farther down, the river reverts to its normal runoff characteristics, and the fishing deteriorates.

The freestone and spring-creek categories are useful for an angler to understand, but, as with much else in fly fishing, they are subject to variation and local idiosyncrasies. An understanding of the variable factors is another vital aspect of the fly fisherman's art.

WATER QUALITY

> *Everyone to his own. The bird is in the sky, the stone rests on land, in water lives the fish....*
> —Angelus Silensius, *The Cherubic Wanderer*

Angelus Silesius may not be a household name, but there is no denying he has put his finger on an essential point—trout do require water. And not just any old water will do. Trout are particular about where they live. In no necessary order of importance, here are the characteristics that trout look for in water:

Oxygen

Trout need a particularly high level of dissolved oxygen—more than most other fish. Indeed, oxygen is a key ingredient in understanding the trout's environment. Many people associate trout habitat with pristine mountain streams, and for the most part that is an accurate image. And it is partly because these streams are remote from people and industry that they are able to maintain the levels of oxygen that trout require.

The depletion of dissolved oxygen results from a vicious cycle. People create pollutants that rivers and lakes collect. These pollutants may be fertilizers that run off or leach into the water table and find their ways into the rivers, or they may be detergents flushed from homes and businesses. Or they may even be sewage. Fertilizers and detergents have high levels of phosphate. Phosphate is a nutrient that stimulates plant growth in the stream (after all, it is being used as fertilizer). This plant growth proliferates, and some of it dies and is decomposed by microorganisms that live in the water. These microorganisms require oxygen, and so the more decomposition that goes on, the more oxygen is used up. Gradually, the water becomes unsuitable for trout. They can't breathe.

Trout streams do require some plant life, because plants are the basis of the food chain and because they use carbon dioxide during photosynthesis and give off oxygen. But too much plant life strangles the stream, because the use of oxygen for decomposition outstrips the water's ability to replenish its oxygen supply. As with most things in nature, a balance is necessary. Pollutants throw things out of balance.

Pollution or a high concentration of aquatic plants and organisms will therefore deplete a stream's oxygen and discourage trout from living in it. The slower the water moves, the more pronounced this phenomenon can become, and it tends to be worst in lakes. Faster water offers no opportunity for excessive plant life to take hold and grow; it just flushes away.

Moving water is also able to replenish its oxygen levels. The action of riffles and waterfalls and rapids aerates the water. Those picturesque mountain streams that tumble over rocks and down rapids are appealing to trout because of their high levels of oxygen. Of course, the trout need places to shelter from the strong currents, so they prefer pools alongside or below the turbulence where they can reside comfortably and still benefit from the oxygen rush created by the rapids (as well as the from the flow of food that comes tumbling along). According to that logic, you'd expect trout to favor deep pools at the base of waterfalls and rapids, and you'd be correct. Their behavior, after all, is reasonable, given their needs.

Water Temperature

Trout like cold water, for two reasons. First, the colder the water, the higher the level of dissolved oxygen. Second, their metabolism functions at optimal levels in relatively cold water. The range of acceptable water temperatures is from 45 degrees (the point at which they start to feed) up to the mid 70s (at which point they stop active feeding and think about siesta). Optimum water temperature for trout is in the 60-to-65-degree range. (This is a very rough rule, however, because some of the "tailwater" fisheries below western dams, such as the San Juan River in New Mexico or the Colorado below Lake Powell in Arizona, have water temperatures that remain in the 40s throughout the year, and they are very rich fisheries with active and aggressive trout.)

A stream that has a spring or several springs as its source will have generally cooler water, and the temperature will not fluctuate as wildly as it will in a stream that depends entirely on runoff. Spring creeks are, therefore, very congenial environments for trout.

Water temperature is affected by the sun, of course, and also by the level of plant life not only in the stream but also above it. Trees and bushes that line the stream and cast shade protect the water from the sun. For that reason, anglers are concerned about logging activities around their favorite streams and rivers, for not only is clear-cutting unsightly, it also reduces the shade available and therefore raises stream temperatures, which in turn reduces oxygen levels and adversely affects the metabolism of the cold-loving trout. Furthermore, the loss of trees (and their root systems) in a river drainage reduces the ability of the ground to hold water, resulting in faster runoff during rainy periods. Floods then carry with them much of the soil that otherwise would have been held in place by the root systems of trees. (Desert rivers are good examples of this phenomenon. In winter when there are rains and mountain snowmelt runoff, the streambeds are brown torrents, but the rest of the year they are bone-dry.) When floods are violent, the trout's habitat gets washed away—along with everyone else's.

Plants in the stream also affect water temperature. They use the sunlight for photosynthesis, and therefore absorb, in a sense, solar energy that would otherwise generate heat. Plants along the bottom of a stream protect the rocks and gravel from direct sunlight, and thereby prevent them from absorbing and retaining heat. But since too much plant life adversely affects oxygen levels, there is a delicate balance to be maintained here. The best types of plants for trout streams are the long, trailing weeds that are common to spring creeks, as opposed to clogging algal matter that proliferates rapidly and ultimately strangles the water.

Acidity and Alkalinity

Anyone with a swimming pool or a memory of chemistry class knows that the pH of water refers to its relative level of acidity or alkalinity. A pH of 7 means that the water is balanced between acids and bases and is, therefore, neutral. Any reading below 7 means the water is acidic. Any reading above 7 means that it's alkaline. Trout can tolerate a fairly wide range of acidity/alkalinity; they can live in water anywhere from 9.5 pH alkalinity to 4.5 pH acidity. Beyond those extremes, they die.

While they can tolerate a fairly wide range, they prefer slightly alkaline water—not because it's inherently more comfortable, but because as a rule it's richer in the nutrients that nourish the insects and crustaceans trout feed on. Alkaline water is simply a richer environment.

Water becomes acidic or alkaline for a variety of reasons (pollution such as acid rain being an obvious cause). A major factor is the character of the countryside through which the stream flows. When a stream flows through an area rich in limestone or chalk deposits, the water becomes alkaline. The pH rises to the mid 8s. The result is a stream that has abundant trout food and many—and generally large—trout. The famous "chalk streams" in southern England, the Test and the Itchen, are examples of this phenomenon, as are the limestone streams of the Eastern United States, such as Pennsylvania's Letort.

Clarity

Trout prefer water that is free from silt, because silt clogs their gills and makes it hard for them to breathe. Silt comes from a number of sources. Natural runoff will, of course, bring with it some silt, but the real problems come from irrigation systems that divert water from one section of the stream and then return it farther down— after it has washed over the farmer's fields. When it's returned to the stream, either directly or through seepage, it has acquired some fertilizers and some silt, and neither is very welcome—at least not from the trout's perspective. Dams are also collectors of silt. As a river flows through a countryside, it naturally picks up some silt. The more it's used for irrigation, the more silt it will collect. Under normal circumstances, that would not be too damaging, since the river would flush the silt out of the area and eventually dump it along its route (during a flood, for instance, when the river runs over its banks) or deposit it into an ever-growing delta system, such as that at the mouth of the Mississippi. But when a dam intervenes, the river stops flowing and the silt settles to the bottom. Periodically, it has to be dredged out.

Dams are controversial subjects for people interested in the environment, but in one way they can create a benefit for trout fishermen. The tailwaters of a dam—the waters just below the dam— are often very productive, for several reasons. First, they are relatively free of silt, since much of it is being collected by the dam. Second, the water flow is managed and therefore less likely to be subject to extreme flows that wash away a trout's habitat and flush the trout itself downstream. Third, many dams release water from below. The water doesn't run over the top of such a dam except during extreme flooding, in which case it's everybody for himself. The water released from below is the coldest in the reservoir, and is therefore ideal for the trout's metabolism and for the levels of dissolved oxygen.

To summarize, trout like cold, clear, non-acidic water that is rich in plant and insect life but not clogged with algae. They like tumbling mountain rivers or spring-fed woodland streams that are well oxygenated and aren't polluted by acid from above or by fertilizers or mud and silt or waste. They can tolerate old cans and tires, but those things usually betoken the human touch which brings other, less tolerable detritus with it.

Sadly, not many rivers and streams meet the trout's requirements. Someone estimated that only about 1 percent of the streams and rivers in the United States support trout. The other rivers and streams lack something that trout need, either for natural reasons or because humanity has made mistakes with the water. Trout thrive where the water is clear and cold, and where the streams are far from industry and urban areas. That's part of the reason anglers seek out trout: our criteria for what makes life worth living are very similar.

Food

One generation passeth away, and another generation cometh: but the earth abideth forever. The sun also ariseth.

—Ecclesiastes

KNOW THAT HEMINGWAY HAS ALREADY USED THESE LINES, but they still work, especially when it comes to the subject of trout food and the insects that are eternally linked with the trout and the fly fisherman—a secular, cyclical trinity.

There is something about trout fishing that seems to impart meaning to anglers and to suggest explanations of things that are otherwise puzzling or depressing. Fly fishing may not be metaphysical, but it is certainly metaphorical, in the sense that its very nature suggests ideas and explanations which are either comforting or useful or both. If that's murky, here's an example. I was sitting in a boat with friend who happens to be a guide, and we were anchored along the bank of the South Fork of the Snake River in Idaho, having lunch. Between this season and the last time I had seen him, he had become a born-again Christian. He wasn't making a big deal about it, but he was curious about my reactions. What, he wanted to know, did I think about the possibilities of the hereafter? I said I didn't have much confidence in my chances, and that I pretty much agreed with Mark Twain that the Heavenly Father had invented the human race because he was disappointed with the monkey. But I added that whenever I thought about these things, which was mostly at night, I also invariably thought about fishing and

about trout flies and about the fact that the insects crawling around on the floor of the South Fork had no idea that at some point in the year they would stop being ugly bugs that spend most of their time clinging to rocks or hiding underneath them and would metamorphose into delicate winged creatures that would spend most of their new incarnation in procreation. That has always struck me as hopeful. The crawling river insects don't have a clue about the good things in store.

People have always used the idea of metamorphosis as a metaphor—or even as a proof of something. And the metamorphosis of aquatic insects—those that interest the trout—is particularly appealing because of the ugliness of the creature at the beginning of the process and the delicate beauty of the final product. Just as the caterpillar turns into a butterfly, so the crawling nymph turns into the winged mayfly. The ugly becomes beautiful, the earthbound becomes airborne, the restrictive physical prison is left behind, and the spirit within is released and flies away. This concept of metamorphosis has always been important in human experience and hopes, and metamorphosis, both as a biological process and an idea, is at the core of the fly fisherman's art. Perhaps that's why fly fishermen tend to be philosophical. Or maybe fly fishing attracts a lot of philosophical people. Or a lot of windbags, take your pick. Certainly there has been more written about fly fishing than about any other sport known to man. It seems not only to fascinate people but also to stimulate the literary glands, and many of the things that have been produced are small gems. Others are not.

It is this hopefulness built into the cycle of things, the rightness of things, that appeals to many fly fishermen, I think. There's a symmetry to the cycle that is comforting and esthetically pleasing at the same time. Everything returns—the seasons, the fish, the insects. Generations change, but the nature of things remains. As Hemingway noted, the sun also rises.

Enough of all that. What about these bugs? There are two things to remember. First, the insects that interest trout and, therefore, fly fishermen live either in the water or along the banks. Those that live in the stream are called aquatic insects, and those that live on the shore are terrestrials. Second, the aquatic insects go through a cycle, a series of changes, and this cycle is really at the heart of the art of fly fishing—and at the heart of the metaphor of fly fishing. (The earlier caveat about generalizations applies here, too, since there are literally thousands of different aquatic insects, and their cycles are not all the same. But they are close enough for most anglers' purposes.)

There is a nice symmetry about the cycle. It revolves around a single year. For fifty-one weeks of that year the typical aquatic insect lives its life as a nymph, and while that may sound romantic, the actual bug is not. Nymphs look sort of like miniature, elongated crabs or lobsters. (And trout regard them with the same relish that we accord the lobster.) Your basic nymph has a hard shell, three legs sticking out each side, two feelers in front, and a three-pronged or forked tail at the back. Nymphs have to shuck the hard outer shell periodically in order to grow. But even when they are relative heavyweights, they measure only an inch or so, at the most. Some nymphs eat the tiny organisms called diatoms which populate the organic matter covering the rocks and the weeds along the bottom of the stream. Others eat vegetation, and still others are predators.

Different nymphs take different approaches to the business of staying alive. Some spend their time clinging to rocks. Others burrow into the bottom of the stream and hide out. Others crawl around on the bottom. Finally, some swim around, hunting and being hunted. Regardless of their particular survival tactics, there comes a time in the life of a nymph when some signal tells it that the time has come to change, to move into a new incarnation, a new form. This is the start of the "hatch." During the hatch, the nymph makes its way to the surface of the water, either by swimming or floating up to the surface or by crawling up the side of the stream. In any event, when it reaches the surface it must break through the surface tension, the invisible skim that covers any water like Saran Wrap on a bowl of leftovers. Breaking through this tension is no easy trick, and it may take the nymph several tries before it succeeds. And while the nymph is struggling to break through (not all of them succeed), it's floating downstream, just under the surface—tempting fate and trout. Different streams, by the way, have different surface-tension characteristics. Spring creeks, with their smooth water, have stronger surface tension than runoff streams in which the tension is broken by the action of riffles. This disruption of the surface tension allows more nymphs to struggle through the surface and hatch.

Once the nymph makes it to and through the surface, it breaks out of its nymphal shell, and a new, winged creature emerges. Depending on the particular type of insect, this new fly may rest for a while on the surface of the stream, drying its wings, and then fly off. Other types will fly off almost immediately. But in any case, there is a period during which the winged insects are floating on the surface of the stream. Then, once they get airborne, they fly to the bushes along the side of the stream, where the males and the females get down to the business of procreation. For the next several days, the insects are romantically engaged, after which the female deposits the now-fertilized eggs in the stream, either by dropping them or by landing briefly on the surface and releasing them. (The technical term for this is "ovipositing.")

Having achieved their mission of perpetuation, the adult flies, males and female both, die. Some aquatic insects, such as the mayfly, die almost immediately. Others may linger for a few weeks, but none lasts more than a month or two after hatching. Many of these dead insects fall onto the surface of the stream, where they float with the current downstream to the feeding stations of the trout, and the trout perfectly understand this whole process. The insect eggs, meanwhile, have sunk to the bottom of the stream and, in the fullness of time (about two weeks), they will develop into small nymphs. And so the cycle begins again.

A good rule of thumb is that the cycle operates over a one-year period from eggs to nymphs to hatch to procreation and finally death. The vast majority of that time (say, fifty-one weeks) is spent as a nymph. With some, their moment in the sun and air lasts just a day—rather short for all the time they put in clinging to underwater rocks. The good times pass quickly for aquatic insects. But they are intensely good, we must assume.

Different species hatch at different times of the year. Bear in mind that there are thousands of different kinds of aquatic insects, each following this basic nymph-through-hatch-through-procreation cycle, but each following its own calendar. Some invariably arrive in the spring, others throughout the summer, still others in the fall. In spring creeks, which have a fairly constant temperature throughout the year, hatches may occur all year round.

Although different insects hatch at different times on the stream, during the warmer months there is usually something hatching at some time during the day. Some hatches are fairly predictable on some streams, but several variables affect the exact timing of the hatch. Warmth (relative warmth, since insects hatch during cooler months, too) seems to be the key. As the day warms up, the rising  temperature triggers the hatch. Also, the sun on the surface of the water affects the fly's behavior. If the sun is beating down, the flies can dry their wings and warm up their flight equipment quickly, and so they get airborne after only a short float downstream. On cloudy days, they might float longer—and in so doing expose themselves longer to the trout waiting for them in the current lines; in essence, the flies run (or float) a longer gantlet before they can dry their wings sufficiently to escape into the air.

And trout are definitely waiting. The flies, whether in their nymphal or winged incarnations, are a key to the trout's diet. Trout will eat other things, too, including small fry and land-based ("terrestrial") insects that fall into the stream. But the aquatic insect that lives and hatches and dies in and on the stream is a staple of the trout's diet, and therefore a key to fly fishing. Indeed, it is precisely because of these insects that the sport is called fly fishing.

The basic cycle, then, starts with the nymph and moves through the hatch, during which the nymph rises to the surface, breaks free of its outer shuck, and emerges as a winged adult that mates, deposits the eggs in the stream, and dies.

But that cycle varies, depending on the type of insect. There are three categories of aquatic insects that are most important to the fly fisherman: the mayflies, the caddisflies, and the stoneflies. Each category—"order," in biology-speak—contains seemingly countless numbers of species. For our purposes, it's not necessary to go beyond the three orders. But it is important to understand the differences.

MAYFLIES

The mayfly is the insect most anglers think about first when they think of fly fishing. It is the most delicate looking fly when mature, and perhaps the most beautiful, especially when not viewed through magnification. The mayfly's scientific name is Ephemeroptera, and I mention that because it's a lovely word and because it describes the essential nature of the mayfly—its ephemeral, fleeting temporality.

The mayfly goes through the cycle of nymph-emerger-adult, but it adds a twist or two which can be important to the angler. First, the nymph floats to the surface using an air sac that develops at the signal to hatch. Those nymphs lucky enough to break through the surface tension of the water then emerge from their nymphal shells. Some species of mayfly start their emergence from the shell on the way up, but the key is that there is a period of final emergence on the surface. (Most of the time, anyway; a few mayflies reach the surface by climbing up rocks that protrude above the water.)

When the winged insect is finally free of the nymphal shell, it must dry its wings for a few moments, or longer—depending on the weather. At this stage, the freshly emerged winged insect is

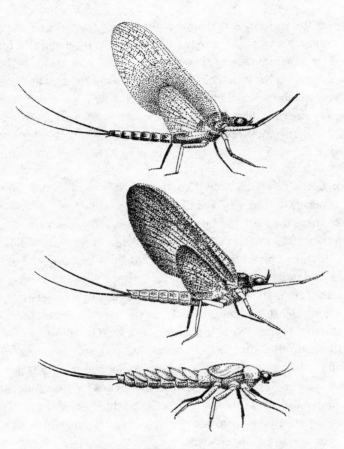

Bottom to top: a mayfly nymph, dun, and spinner. All three stages are eaten by trout; the importance of each stage varies according to the species of mayfly.

called a dun. From the moment of the hatch, the mayfly ceases to eat, and so the deeper it goes into the final stages of the cycle, the less nutritious the fly becomes, as it burns up its energy in the final mad stages of its wooing. As the dun floats on the surface, its wings held upright like the sails on a small yacht, it is obviously a target for the trout, and it is common knowledge among anglers that a major hatch is generally a signal for trout to start to feed aggressively on the surface. It is then that fly fishing reaches one of its most dramatic stages—a frenzy of activity for the trout and also for the angler, who often loses his normal *sang-froid* as he stands in the stream or on the bank watching fish rising all around him and trying, with trembling hands, to tie on a fly that he hopes resembles the newly emerged duns. The scene resonates among all fly fishermen; Norman Rockwell even painted it for the cover of the *Saturday Evening Post*, thereby enshrining "The Angler and the Hatch" in American iconography.

Not all the newly hatched duns float to their doom, obviously. Many manage to take wing and fly to the bushes and trees along the banks. There they go through another transition—a molt during which they shed what's called an exoskeleton, a secondary outer shell which had protected the mayfly dun from becoming waterlogged during its initial travails on the surface. Once in the trees and bushes along the shore, the dun discards this now unnecessary protection, and in so doing reveals, in the case of the male, his reproductive organs. Now the male is ready. (One thinks of the Crusader returning after years in the Holy Land, struggling out of his armor while his lady waits.) This newly molted mayfly is now called a spinner. Spinners are brightly colored and have translucent (or even transparent) wings, whereas the duller-colored dun's wings were covered with an opaque protective coating, which now, like his armor, is no longer needed.

Spruced up by the molt, the spinner is ready to make up for those long solitary days as a nymph. What's more, the spinner is a stripped-down, lean mean flying machine. His molt not only released his reproductive equipment but also reduced him down to the essentials, which means that he can now fly with Concorde-like efficiency—the better to avoid airborne predators. (I have seen literally thousands of violet-green swallows hunting above the surface of the San Juan River—so many that we actually hooked two of them, which we released unharmed, and hit many more with the fly line. To run that sort of gantlet, the mayfly spinner needs to be nimble in the air.)

Then follows a mass marriage in the swarm of insects above the stream and along the banks. Mating takes place in the air. Like many other creatures, the mayfly seems to prefer to do his wooing in the late afternoon and evening, and may extend festivities well into the night. The males, also not uniquely, may mate with several females. While their erstwhile mates are being untrue to them, the mated females deposit their newly fertilized eggs in the stream, according to their preferred methods of ovipositing. When the festivities are over, the females and the males expire—they are truly exhausted—and the result is called the spinner fall. The dead spinners float downstream, their translucent wings now limp at their sides. Trout will often take these dead flies, although they understand that the spinners have used up much of their energy—and therefore their nutritional value—in the act of reproducing themselves, and so the trout may not feed on them with as much relish as they exhibit in capturing the more succulent duns. Here again, though, the rule about generalizations applies: many spinner falls produce excellent angling.

So here's the mayfly cycle: When it's crawling along the stream bottom or hiding under a rock and wearing a hard outer shell, the creature is called a nymph. When it's swimming to the surface and struggling first to break through the surface tension and then to rid itself of its shell, it's called an emerger. Once the mayfly has emerged and the winged insect is floating along the surface, it's called a dun. Then, from the time when it sits in the bushes and develops its sexual capability through the time when it mates and dies, it's called a spinner. Only the mayfly goes through these two stages as an winged adult—the dun and the spinner phase. The spinners mate, the eggs are deposited, and the game is done, sometimes all in a single day. And it is the idea of the spinner—a creature solely designed for love that dies of exhaustion immediately after fulfilling its role—that appeals to so many anglers, even silent, scientific anglers and amateur entomologists who know the Latin names of the various mayfly species. The mayfly's cycle is irresistibly romantic—delicate, doomed, airborne lovers.

CADDISFLIES

The caddisflies constitute the second broad category of aquatic insects. Their scientific name is Trichoptera. Whereas the exquisite mayfly is the aristocrat of the aquatic insects, at least in terms of its position in the hearts and minds of most anglers, the caddisfly is a sturdy burgher, a stout, moth-like bug with a no-nonsense approach to the business of hatching and procreation. In England, the motherland of fly fishing, caddis are called sedges, a utilitarian name that reflects their approach to life: "sedge" is also the name of the grass along the banks.

The caddis resembles a moth in that its wings fold down over the insect's body when at rest, whereas the mayfly's resting wings stand up like the sail on a schooner. According to entomologists, caddisflies are actually a higher order of insects than mayflies, regardless of conventional angling opinion. Their higher status stems from the fact that they undergo a complete metamorphosis—from larva to pupa to winged adult—while the mayflies do not bother with the pupal stage and go from nymph directly to the winged phase. A pupa is a larva that has built a cocoon and undergone a physical transformation. While the larva looks rather like a worm, the pupa is a stocky bug with large eyes and antennae. When it's time to hatch, the pupa breaks out of the cocoon and moves to the surface.

The caddis, in other words, has two underwater phases: the larval and pupal stages. At some point in its cycle, the larva receives a signal that it's time to build a case, or cocoon. It does so, and during its encasement it develops into a pupa. When the pupa receives its inward signal to hatch, it swims to the surface, breaks out of the pupal shuck, and almost immediately flies off the surface. Caddis, in other words, make the transition to winged adult without wasting any time; they do not need to tarry on the surface to dry their wings or to warm their flight muscles. They arrive at the surface ready to break out of their shucks, and when they do they are also virtually ready to fly. Trout understand the process, and they know that if they see a floating caddis, it can mean two things—either that caddis is real, in which case it will take off quickly, and so it had better be eaten even more quickly, or it's not really a caddis and should be avoided because a caddis won't drift for long periods.

People who fish caddisfly imitations successfully will generally duplicate this fly's behavior by dapping the surface with the fly— touching down briefly, picking up, touching down again, picking up, and so on. Of course, here again the law of generalization applies. Because trout wait in feeding stations, they don't always see flies floating for long distances. That means, if you're floating a caddis imitation and if it's floating naturally in the current, a trout in a feeding station may see it for only a short time and may therefore conclude that it's acting naturally. And, of course, the more riffled the surface is, the less opportunity the trout has to see and study the fly. All generalizations are false, including this one.

Unlike the romantic mayflies, caddis make love on the ground, along the banks of the stream—presumably after a picnic consisting of plant juice, which is the caddisfly's idea of lobster and cham-

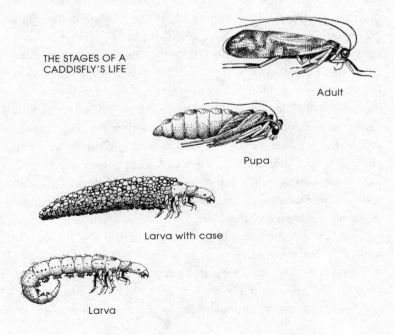

THE STAGES OF A
CADDISFLY'S LIFE

Adult

Pupa

Larva with case

Larva

pagne. Trichoptera do share the mayfly's preference for evening trysts. They dislike strong light at any time, and are most active on cloudy days and in the evening hours. And they will do a bit of swarming above the stream before pairing off in the bushes. When mating has been completed, the female flies to the stream and deposits her eggs either by dipping several times onto the surface of the water or by diving under the surface to attach the eggs to plants or rocks. Caddis live rather long compared to mayflies—they might last as long as two months—and there is no dramatic, swooning spinner fall with these sturdy burghers. In fact, there are no spinners at all, since that is a term—and a phenomenon—reserved for the mayfly.

STONEFLIES

At the risk of forcing the sociological metaphors too far, stoneflies might be described as the thick-necked proletariat of the aquatic insects. Their order has the scientific name Plecoptera. Like the mayflies, their metamorphosis is "incomplete," because they develop from egg to nymph to winged adult without passing through a pupal stage. Even more pedestrian, rather than swimming or floating to the surface of the stream, stonefly nymphs crawl out of the water when it comes time to hatch. They may labor up the side of the stream onto the land or they may crawl onto a branch or rock in the stream. But the key is that their emergence as winged adults takes place out of the water. When stoneflies are hatching, anglers and other interested parties will find the stonefly shucks scattered along the banks of the stream. They look like the pale, plastic, hollow insects that you sometimes see in drugstores around Halloween. Since they hatch on dry surfaces, stoneflies dislike strong sunlight, because the drying action of the sun may harden the nymphal shell and make it difficult or impossible for the adult to break free. For this reason, stoneflies often hatch in the evening or at night. The life cycle of the stonefly varies by species, but the same useful rule of thumb that applies to mayflies also applies here—a one-year cycle from egg to nymph to adult. Some species take more than a year to mature. Interestingly, stoneflies hatch throughout the year, even in winter, depending again on the species.

Stoneflies need highly oxygenated and unpolluted water, and their presence in a stream is a good sign for more than one reason—it means that the stream is pure and also that trout are likely to be present. Whether as nymphs or adults, stoneflies tend to be large, very tempting morsels which trout take eagerly. But esthetically, they are something of a failure. The nymphs resemble mayfly nymphs (no beauties themselves), but they are slightly larger and, when magnified, more menacing-looking, like a monster in a Japanese sci-fi movie. Some stonefly nymphs, notably the golden and yellow species, sport strikingly mottled color schemes. When hatched into a winged adult, the stonefly has two sets of wings which fold down over its body when at rest, so that the casual observer might easily mistake the insect for a cockroach. Or worse.

In flight, the stoneflies are more graceful than on land; and unlike the mayflies and caddis, which fly with their bodies parallel to the water, stoneflies keep their bodies perpendicular to the surface, so they are easy to recognize in flight. Also, they have two sets of equal-sized wings. And while stoneflies tend to be larger and uglier than the other orders of aquatic insects, there are some delicate blond species that rival any mayfly debutante. Their relatively large size makes them especially attractive to trout, which are not concerned with beauty but with calories. One dash to the surface yields a major return for the trout's investment of energy. And since stoneflies are a favorite of trout, they are a favorite of anglers.

The stonefly mates on land, and in his only attempt at cutting a romantic figure, the male jackhammers his hard abdomen against a rock or something and makes a noise which is similar in purpose to the drumming of a male ruffed grouse. Both displays have the object of attracting a female. The female deposits her eggs in a variety of ways: dropping them into the stream from the air, diving into the stream, or skittering across the surface in a kind of mad ovipositing dash that may remind some people of a merganser trying to get airborne.

Stoneflies' life spans are more like those of caddisflies than mayflies, since stoneflies can live as adults for as long as a month. There is no spinner phase and therefore no spinner fall for stoneflies.

DRIFTING ALONG

Mayfly and stonefly nymphs, and caddisfly larvae and pupae all live under the surface, on the bottom of the stream. Some live under rocks, others burrow, and so on. But every day, usually in periods of low light, some of these creatures go wandering. This is called the "drift." Whether they do this voluntarily or because they are being swept downstream depends on the conditions in the stream. In periods of flood, the increased volume of water will wash some of these insects downstream. But interestingly, when water levels drop there is also an increased drift. Some scientists therefore assume that drift is a way in which these creatures get a little elbow room, which they need to avoid overcrowding and the resultant strain on food and living space. And when the water levels are dropping, the insects are apparently trying to avoid being trapped in a puddle or marooned high and dry.

In any case, whether by flood or by choice, the insects drift downstream every day, under the surface. The variations on this phenomenon are huge, depending again on the species. Sometimes they may go only a few feet. At other times, and among other species, the drift may be the length of a football field. The point for fly fishermen is that something is generally moving in the stream; insects are hatching, others are drifting. There is a lot activity in the insect world beneath the surface.

WHAT ELSE IS ON THE MENU?

Mayflies, caddisflies, and stoneflies are the three major groups that interest fly fishermen, but trout do eat other things. The number and variety of these alternatives to the big three are so great that the best course of action is just to touch on the ones that are most commonly replicated with trout flies.

Dragonflies and Damselflies

Everyone knows what a dragonfly looks like. Well, a damselfly looks essentially the same except that it holds its wings over its back when at rest, whereas a dragonfly keeps its wings straight out when not using them. Dragonflies are a little sturdier-looking than damselflies—bigger, thicker. If the damselfly is a ballerina, the dragonfly is a field-hockey goalie. Both are aquatic insects in the sense that they lay their eggs in the water and go through a metamorphosis similar to that of the stonefly—nymph to winged adult without passing through a pupal stage. These nymphs are most important to the trout, and some live as long as four years in the nymphal stage. A variety of damselfly-nymph patterns have been devised, and they take many trout in lakes and weedy streams.

Flies imitating an adult dragonfly are generally bodies tied on long-shanked hooks, and they are fished most often on lakes where the angler simply throws the fly near a lily pad and lets it sit motionless until a trout decides to eat it. I have never seen a fly tied to imitate a winged adult, although someone somewhere must have tied one, if only for the fun of it. Since these adults are relatively large, it would be difficult to cast the fly. More importantly, these bugs are not habitués of a stream surface, and so they are not typical trout food except as nymphs. That is not to say that a trout will not rise up and snatch a dragonfly that is daydreaming near the water surface. It's just not that common because these flies don't generally hang around the stream in large numbers.

Diptera

Diptera means "two wings," and it is a huge order that includes some of the least popular creatures on earth—mosquitoes, gnats, midges, blackflies, deerflies, horseflies, houseflies and about 85,000 other species of dubious reputation. The larvae of these insects are, if possible, even more unattractive than the adults; they are called maggots. A few of the diptera are aquatic insects in the sense that they lay their eggs in the water and go through a complete metamorphosis—larva, pupa, adult.

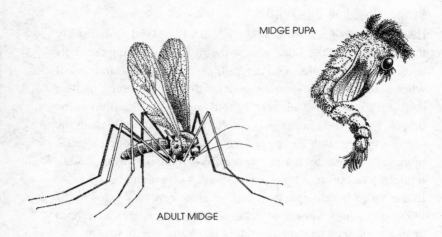

MIDGE PUPA

ADULT MIDGE

Of all the diptera, the midge is probably the only adult fly that interests the angler, because trout will feed on the adult midge, even though doing so defies logic to some extent. It would hardly seem to be worth the effort to eat these tiny bugs, but for some reason trout like them, and many a nearsighted fly fisherman has cursed these little creatures (and the trout's fondness for them) as he tries, arms fully extended, to thread a delicate monofilament leader through a tiny eye of a tiny hook of a midge imitation. Even more maddening is a hatch of midges which the trout seem to be feeding on but which in fact they are ignoring, since they are actually feeding on emerging midges just below the surface. The trout create surface disturbances as they take these emergers and in so doing delude the angler into thinking that an imitation of an adult midge is the answer.

Despite their diminutive size, midges can be a key item of food for trout. The water just below the Glen Canyon Dam in northern Arizona is primarily midge water (along with some scuds and small worms), and the rainbows there are large and athletic despite their reliance on the midge. Interestingly, there do not seem to be any mayflies, caddis, or stoneflies in that water, but the trout are thriving nonetheless.

Worms

These are not nightcrawlers or earthworms or similar beauties, which are best reserved for small boys to dangle in front of girls and for bait fishermen. No, these are aquatic worms that will be revealed if you shuffle your feet on the bottom of some streams. They're about an inch long, thin, and sometimes brightly colored. Trout like them. Of course, trout also like earthworms, but dunking a real worm is beyond the pale.

Crustaceans

Shrimps and crayfish—now we're talking. Finally something on the menu that makes sense to a human.

The "shrimps" are not really shrimps, though, but rather scuds. People call them freshwater shrimps anyway. They run up to an inch in length, with arched bodies (though they are straight when swimming or drifting) and numerous legs sticking down, and they seem particularly to like the weedbeds of spring creeks. That's one more reason why trout like to hang in these weedbeds: tempting shrimp cocktails served in an environment free from obstreperous currents and yet well protected from most predators. Stare at these weedbeds waving in the gentle currents long enough and one of the weed stems will turn out to be a trout whose matching coloring and ability to synchronize his quiet movements with the weeds make the fish well-nigh invisible even in the clear water. It may only be when he dashes forward to pluck a scud from the weeds that we can see him.

Crayfish, as every Cajun food aficionado knows, can get pretty big—up to six inches. Trout, especially big trout, like them as much as any human. The bigger the trout, the bigger the meal he needs in order to keep going. Moreover, as a trout grows he spends more and more of his time eating below the surface of the water. Really big trout—those over five pounds—rarely feed on surface insects, and these big fish are the fellows that are particularly partial to crayfish. Like any crustacean, crayfish have to molt their hard shells in order to grow, and they are particularly attractive to trout during the period just after the molt, for the same reason that humans like soft-shell crabs: there's no need to bother getting past the shell—just dip in the sauce and have at it.

Other Fish and Leeches

When it comes to ugly, few fish surpass the sculpin. It is a bottom-dwelling, small fish that looks like a miniature version of a grouper, only not so handsome. It has outsized fins, dull coloring, and an oversized flat head. It's a primitive-looking creature. Trout like sculpins, for they make a good meal for trout of almost any size. They're big enough to attract really large trout, yet small enough to be caught even by a juvenile member of the trout clan. Despite their uncouth appearance, sculpins have very refined standards for habitat. They require cold, pure water that is rich in oxygen. They therefore coexist quite well with trout, which of course require the same sort of living conditions.

The other key fish that trout relish is the dace. A dace is essentially a minnow. These little fish school around in the shallows looking for food and trying to avoid becoming food. The Black-nosed Dace is a popular trout fly, because the real thing is a popular food item for trout. It makes a good meal since, like the sculpin, a dace is a couple of inches long and therefore worth the effort of chasing and chewing.

Is a leech a fish? Hardly, but trout don't care. They eat them. Most people think of leeches in a rather uncomplimentary way— if someone called you a leech, you would not be flattered. But to a trout they are well worth having to dinner. They travel around the stream looking for something to attach themselves to, since they are parasites. (I have seen them attached to mallard ducks, and they are extremely tough and hard to smash.) Trout will eat them readily, though, with no problems of digestion. I mention these creatures primarily because the trout like them and because there are therefore some very useful trout flies which are tied to imitate them.

Terrestrials

Terrestrials, as the name implies, are insects and other creatures that normally live on land, but, for a variety of reasons, suddenly find themselves afloat in a trout stream. Being land-based, they generally are poor swimmers, and they are certainly unfamiliar with the problems of surface tension and current. They therefore tend to flutter or struggle on the surface, and that often has the effect of attracting predators, such as trout, but has no real effect on their ability to get out of their watery predicament. The terrestrials may be blown into the stream by the wind or washed into it by rain and flooding, or they may not be paying attention as they wander along the bank and so fall into the water. Terrestrials are therefore not a regular or reliable source of food, but they are important targets of opportunity for trout. In fact, it may well be that because their appearance is both familiar and yet unexpected, they are especially attractive to trout—a surprise variation on the everyday menu.

Grasshoppers are among the most welcome of the insects that blunder into a stream. Large and juicy, they tend to find themselves waterborne during hot, sunny, and breezy days when the heat of the sun gets them moving around on shore and wind blows them off the grassy banks into the current—or when they jump to the left when they should have jumped to the right. As you might expect, hoppers tend to fall in fairly close to the shore. Also lying close to the shore are trout whose idea of a perfect residence is the undercut bank of a stream, a place where they can hide from predators by holding underneath the bank and at the same time see insects borne in the current lines that parallel the bank (the very current lines that have carved the undercut). Grasshoppers that fall into these locations will never see the land again, and they will not float far. In fact, many trout like to hold close to the bank, whether below an undercut bank or just offshore where the bottom drops off into greater depth. In either case, they're close to the current lines which are often just a few feet from the shore, and it's just the kind of place where hoppers fall or get blown.

Ants are even more popular with trout, it seems. That may seem unreasonable, since they're so small, but trout seem to love them. Someone has suggested that trout just like the taste of them, which is a good enough explanation. Most people would rather eat a peanut than a Brussels sprout, so we're all in agreement that taste generally matters more than volume.

Ants don't necessarily need any assistance from the wind or weather to end up in the water. They just seem to fall into the stream in enough numbers to keep the trout interested. Like grasshoppers, they are not very good swimmers, but they are pretty good floaters. That means they make a very good trout fly, because trout are accustomed to seeing real ants caught in the surface tension and current, floating along until they're eaten, drowned, or washed up on a rock or tree branch.

Other land-based insects such as beetles and bees make an occasional visits to trout waters, and if you go to a fly shop, you'll see some imitations of these bugs. I would suggest having a heart-to-heart talk with the shop owner about local conditions before investing in these kinds of flies, though. Hoppers and ants, yes, definitely. They are very important in anyone's fly box. More exotic beetles and such, I don't know. Those are the things you might want to experiment with on days that are slow. And there are such days. Scientists who have done studies of the contents of trout stomachs do find bees now and then.

Some fly shops also carry frog and even small mouse imitations. These are primarily used for bass. (By the way, they can be very good for bass, and bass can be very good for fly fishermen.) Trout fishermen don't generally use such things, because trout generally don't seem to be interested in them. Perhaps they're too big for the trout that generally feed on the surface and too far away from the monstrous brutes hunting in the deep holes. I'm sure that big trout do take a swimming mouse now and then, and a swimming frog as well, but these flies are generally not used by trout anglers—not from any strong prejudice against them, but because, I suspect, the likelihood of raising a good fish is a lot greater using other kinds of flies. And, in truth, there may be a bit of snobbishness at work as well.

As a rule, trout will eat just about anything that is protein and in the water—and the bigger the fish, the more he needs. But many fly fishermen would be happier taking a big fish on a more traditional fly than, say, on a mouse. It lacks a certain *je ne sais quoi*. Plus, they're big, hairy, and hard to cast, so you need a bigger fly rod—one with dimensions that might not be suitable for a trout stream.

Speaking of fly shops brings us to the next logical subject—the flies an angler buys or ties. We've talked about the kinds that are real; now it's time to talk about the kinds that are made of thread and fur and feathers and come with hooks.

Trout Flies

*They fashion red wool around a hook and fix on to the
wool two feathers and which in color are like wax.
Their rod is six feet long and their line the same
length. Then they throw their snare, and the fish, mad-
dened and excited by the color, come straight at it,
thinking by the sight to get a dainty mouthful; when,
however, it opens its jaws, it is caught by the hook and
enjoys a bitter repast, a captive.*

—Aelian, circa A.D. 200
(as quoted in Conrad Voss Bark's *A History of Flyfishing*)

ELIAN WAS A SPANIARD WHO LIVED IN ROME. He had an
interest in natural history, and the quotation is taken
from his description of Macedonian fishing techniques.
So, not only did the Macedonians give us Alexander the Great, they
also gave us the first recorded examples of dry-fly fishing, that is,
fishing an imitation of an insect floating on the surface of the water.
(And since they did not bother to give their fly a name, I suggest
"Bitter Red Repast" as a possibility.) Aelian was a reporter rather
than an angler, and we must take his explanation of the process
with a grain of salt. He expresses, however, ideas which persist to
this day—the emphasis on color, for example. No one would seriously dispute that the color of a fly affects its ability to attract trout;
though anglers differ about the importance of color compared to
size, design, fly selection, and other depths we will plumb later.

We can draw two conclusions from Aelian's description of
Macedonian fly fishing. First, people have been at this game a long
time. In fact, there are references in Homer to techniques of fish-

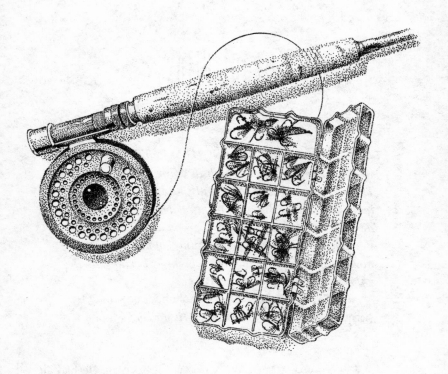

ing with a feather and hook, a fly designed to resemble a minnow rather than an insect. Homer wrote in the ninth century B.C. about the Trojan War, which as far as anyone can determine took place around the fifteenth century B.C., so we can assume that people have been trying to fool fish with flies at least from the time of Achilles and Ulysses. For some reason, that is a deeply satisfying thought. (This information may lead to new interpretations of Homer's work. Consider the famous line: "By their own follies they perished, the fools." Could he have been referring to trout rather than to ancient warriors?) These Homeric flies were wet flies, meaning they were fished below the surface of the water. Aelian's Bitter Red Repast, however, was a dry fly, meaning it was supposed to float. Since the Macedonians did not have the modern angler's access to many materials, the fly probably did not float very long. More than likely, the angler crouched in the bushes on the bank and held the fly on the surface by using a rod and a very short line. The fly probably became waterlogged quickly, and the angler would have picked it up after a few seconds and dropped it down again—a technique modern anglers call "dapping." But it was dry-fly fishing, nonetheless.

The second important implication of Aelian's text is that people were using artificial flies because these flies worked. People were not fly fishing in those days because it was fashionable, but rather because it was the most effective way to catch trout that were taking insects off the surface of the water. Undoubtedly the Macedonians tried at first to skewer real insects on their hooks, but the delicate mayflies and caddis were either too small or too fragile to stay on a hook for long, and the ancient anglers had to find a better way. They turned to making and using artificial flies.

So fly fishing is a technique that is both venerable and effective.

But what exactly is a fly—not the insect, but the lure? There are many different answers to that question, but fortunately we are interested in trout fishing so the answer is relatively straightforward. A trout fly is an arrangement of feathers and fur (and often other materials) tied around a hook. A fly fisherman, in short, deals only in artifice and artificials. Fly fishermen do not use bait, which is something that either is, or at one time was, alive; nor do they use metal spoons or molded plastic imitations of minnows or (gasp) rubbery worms or cheeseballs or salmon eggs. (Fly fishermen, however, do not sneer at using yarn *imitations* of salmon eggs. The distinction may seem Jesuitical to an outsider, but it is very real and important to anglers; the gulf between someone who would use a real salmon egg and a fly fisherman who would only use an imitation salmon egg is almost unbridgeable.) Beyond those restrictions, however, the definition of a fly is pretty broad: a collection of materials tied by hand onto a hook. Sometimes a legitimate fly is not even tied: I have used epoxy crab flies for bonefish, and these heavy objects are molded around the shank of the hook. They certainly are not "tied" in the normal sense of the word.

There are two types of trout flies—those that imitate natural insects or other prey and those that are products of human imagination, look like nothing natural on earth, and are designed to appeal to the trout's culinary curiosity or to stimulate his aggressiveness. In other words, there are the *imitations* and the *attractors*. Imitations are to attractors as *trompe l'oeil* paintings are to expressionism. The imitation attempts to fool the eye by duplicating reality; the attractor attempts to entice the eye through an arrangement of colors and materials that doesn't look like anything we can immediately recognize.

In either case, the flies are made of various materials such as feathers, fur, synthetic threads—in fact, a range of materials that seems as vast as the range of mayfly species—and these materials are arranged in designs that are themselves so various as to strain the mental resources of the most dedicated taxonomist. In short, there are lots of fly patterns; every person who has ever tied flies has designed at least one new pattern—sometimes intentionally.

All of these designs, whether natural imitations or attractors, fall into several categories. Here are the basics; bear in mind that these categories apply to both imitations and attractors.

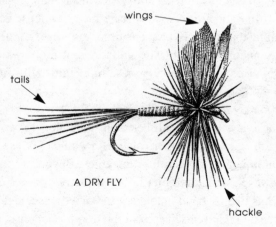

wings

tails

A DRY FLY

hackle

Dry Flies

These are flies designed to float on the surface of the water and so, in most cases, to imitate or suggest newly hatched mayfly duns or spinners or ovipositing females or terrestrials that have just gone astray—or any insect that is floating on the surface. A dry fly is not literally dry, since some part of the fly is in contact with the water. But the key idea to remember is that a dry fly is supposed to float. It rests in the surface tension and rides in the current line. In order to eat it, the trout must rise to the surface. There are also many patterns of dry flies which are attractors—floating flies which are interesting (to trout) arrangements of materials and colors and which therefore entice the trout up for a closer look and, perhaps, a nibble.

Wet Flies

Wet flies swim or drift beneath the surface. The term "wet" has come to refer as much to a technique of fishing a fly as to a type of fly. In other words, people speak about fishing a particular fly "wet," which means they're working the fly below the surface. The term is also used to describe certain flies which imitate emergers—insects which have started to hatch and are moving from the nymphal stage up to the surface, where they will then become duns. Some insects begin the emergence as they float to the surface, so that they have some profile of the adult fly, with their wings, perhaps, out but not yet erect. These are wet flies, too. So, a wet fly refers either to an imitation of an insect that lives beneath the surface or to a technique of fishing any fly below the surface. (Flies that imitate minnows and other subsurface dwellers are also technically wet flies in the sense that they are never fished on the surface, but most anglers call them "streamers," as we will see.)

Nymphs

These are pretty straightforward flies. They're designed to imitate aquatic insects in their nymphal stage, and they're fished wet, since nymphs are generally found beneath the surface. You would not expect to see a nymph floating on the surface, so there is no such thing as dry-fly nymph. Technically, that makes all nymphs wet flies. But not all wet flies are nymphs.

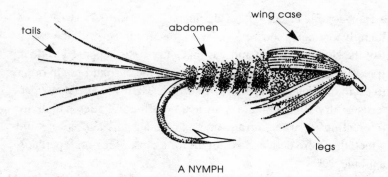

A NYMPH

Streamers

These are flies which are tied to suggest minnows, leeches, sculpins—those denizens of the stream that are not insects. Some of these flies are also called bucktails, because of the materials (the hair of a male deer's tail, for instance) used in tying some of them. They tend to have long, flowing profiles as they move through the water—which would explain the derivation of the term *streamer*. Streamers are generally fished wet, since they represent creatures that live below the surface. Now and then, an angler may skitter a streamer across the surface to imitate a panicky minnow, but that is not dry-fly fishing.

Streamers are wet flies that are fished wet...except when they are fished dry, as in the case, say, of the Muddler Minnow. This is a versatile fly that is designed to be fished wet and thereby imitate

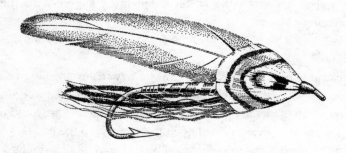

ONE TYPE OF STREAMER

a small fish, but it can be fished dry, since when it floats it very much resembles a grasshopper. The point here is that the terms "wet" and "dry" refer not only to types of flies but also to the method of fishing them. "Wet" means below the surface; "dry" means floating on the surface. In most cases, a wet fly is fished wet and a dry fly dry, but some flies work two jobs.

Regardless of the type of fly, all patterns have individual names. Sometimes these names simply describe the aquatic insect being duplicated, such as the *Callibaetis* Spinner. Other times the names are whimsical, such as the justly famous Rat-Faced McDougal and the less famous, but effective, Green Machine. Then, too, they're sometimes named for their designer, as in the case of the Royal Wulff, which was invented by Lee Wulff. And there is the Quill Gordon, named for Theodore Gordon, the man credited with introducing dry-fly fishing to American anglers. The names of these flies are even more various than the flies themselves, because the same fly might be called something different in different parts of the country. Sometimes a pattern has more than one name in the same part of the country; in Idaho there is a fly called a Yellow Sally and another called a Mormon Girl. Frankly, I can't tell them apart, and I suspect they are the same fly in different moods.

The outdoor writer Gene Hill once admitted that he can't remember the names of a lot of the flies he uses regularly, much less the names of all the other thousands of patterns, so he just goes with titles such as "the brown one with speckled wings." It works just as well. Fly fishing, like heaven, has many mansions, and room for all.

A BRIEF DIGRESSION ON THE GREAT DRY-FLY CONTROVERSY

Speaking of Heaven conjures up the opening lines from Norman Maclean's *A River Runs Through It*:

> In our family, there was no clear line between religion
> and fly fishing. We lived at the junction of great trout

rivers in western Montana, and our father was a Presbyterian minister and a fly fisherman who tied his own flies and taught others. He told us about Christ's disciples being fishermen, and we were left to assume, as my brother and I did, that all the first-class fishermen on the Sea of Galilee were fly fishermen and that John, the favorite, was a dry-fly fisherman.

This lovely paragraph encapsulates one of the abiding myths of fly fishing. It is widely argued that dry-fly fishing is the purest form of the sport. In other words, there is a hierarchy in the world of fishing. At the top of the hierarchy is the fly fisherman, placed there by himself. And at the top of the fly fishermen's peerage resides the dry-fly fisherman, the dry-fly purist.

Why is this so?

First of all, fly fishermen are inveterate classifiers. People who develop and maintain an interest in the various categories of aquatic insects are naturally going to extend this tendency to other forms of endeavor. They will try to arrange human activities into classes, and it is not surprising that when they think about the various kinds of angling, they place their preferred method at the top. In all of this there is, of course, an element of snobbery, an instinct only slightly less powerful than sex.

Fly fishing, wet or dry, is viewed as having more "tone" than other kinds of fishing, because it requires a fair amount of skill, uses equipment that can be costly, revels in arcane information about insects and stream chemistry, and derives most of its traditions and notions of hierarchy from the upper classes of England, who more or less invented modern fly fishing. What's more, the quarry—trout or salmon, usually—resides in out-of-the-way places that are pristinely beautiful (and sometimes expensive to get to). All of this is in stark contrast to a bait fisherman who sits on an inverted plastic bucket and dangles a worm in a canal in hopes of hooking a bluegill.

Human nature being what it is, it is not difficult to see why fly fishing has awarded itself a cachet that separates it and its practitioners from the angling proletariat. But why is *dry*-fly fishing in particular regarded as the purest of the pure, the ultimate expression of the ultimate style of angling? For that answer we need to look at the history of the sport.

In the nineteenth century, the availability of easy train transportation from London meant that people could reach the chalk streams of Hampshire without too much difficulty, fish for a few days, and then return to the city. They could do this throughout the season; it was easy, and so trout fishing became increasingly popular among the upper classes who had the money for equipment, leisure time to use it, and access to the private waters. (In England, virtually all fishing water was privately owned; still is.) Not surprisingly, clubs sprang up. One purpose of the clubs was to maintain the water, since trout streams such as the Test and Itchen were divided into sections, each of which was either owned or leased. Clubs leased some of the water, and they were responsible for maintaining it. To do that, they hired riverkeepers to manage their sections of the streams. That meant keeping the growth of weeds at levels that would stimulate insects and crustaceans but not clog the stream; maintaining the river banks; killing off the predators, such as pike and otters; and making sure no poachers came in the dark of the night and made off with the fish.

Many of these famous streams were chalk streams—smoothwater streams that amble through the pastureland. They were, and are, what we in the U.S. call spring creeks, spring-fed streams with constant flows of water at relatively constant temperatures. They traverse a landscape that is rich in chalk, and the water therefore acquires an alkalinity that stimulates the food chain. The water is flat and the trout live in an extremely agreeable environment, one that allows them to cruise a bit more than their cousins in runoff streams, who must fight the various currents and riffles and must take and keep preferred lies for resting and feeding. The chalk-stream trout were like the men who stalked them—comfortable and well fed.

All of the stream surface in a spring creek looks pretty much the same—no big boulders or rapids or shallows—and therefore it is virtually impossible to determine where a trout might be lurking. It all looks the same. This is very different from a runoff stream, in which the holding and feeding lies are not difficult to spot, once you have the hang of it. In a chalk stream, the only way to determine where a trout is—aside from spotting him holding in the weedbeds—is to see him rising to feed on the surface. The ring or splash the trout makes identifies him as a candidate for the fly. As long as the trout are feeding below the surface, or not feeding at all, it is not easy to spot them. That was especially true in the days before polarizing sunglasses, which reduce surface glare and let modern anglers see fish more easily.

As a result of this natural phenomenon (the normal behavior of trout in a spring creek), the gentlemen anglers of the clubs learned that the best way to catch these trout was to stalk a fish that was rising to natural insects and then to float a dry fly that imitated those naturals over the place where the fish was feeding. Dry-fly fishing, in other words, was the most reasonable way to catch fish on a chalk stream. You were fishing to a known fish whose rises revealed two important things: that he was there and that he was feeding.

Since a feeding fish has his nose in the current, and since he can see you more easily if you are alongside or ahead of him, it makes sense to approach the fish from below, from downstream. That means that if you are fishing dry flies to a rising fish, you are throwing your fly upstream. So chalk-stream fishing at its most effective entailed casting a dry fly upstream to a rising fish.

This perfectly natural response to the conditions on a chalk stream gradually ossified into a code of conduct which acquired a value unto itself. Dry-fly fishing, instead of being seen as an effective means to an end, became an end in itself. The makers of the rules injected themselves into the process and declared that one fished only to a rising fish, a known fish—not because it made the most sense but because it was the "done thing." Anything else was poor form.

Strict rules often create rebellion, and the English fishing community in the nineteenth century had its share of Jacobins. The forces of rebellion were advocates of nymph fishing. They pointed out that trout spend the vast majority of their feeding time (some say 90 percent) eating things under the surface. If the object is to catch trout, these rebels asked, why then should we not fish beneath the surface—fish wet flies and, specifically, nymphs? Why wait until a fish starts to feed on the surface? Weather and wind may ruin a hatch for a day, and the trout may never rise. But they still will feed under the surface. Why waste the day, asked the rebels? Why not send the letter to the current address?

The rebels had some elements of tradition on their side, since most salmon fishing is done with wet flies. (As an aside, all salmon flies are attractors, since salmon, while migrating back to their home waters to spawn, do not eat en route. Why they bother to strike at these attractors is a question that is still debated.) What's more, the *earliest* English trout flies were wet flies. Dry flies as we think of them today were a relatively new idea in England. In other words, the wet-fly rebels were not advocating something completely unknown in the angling world. The rebels went on to say that they could still fish to a known fish, since the clarity of the water was such that, with care, they could spot a fish in the weeds and swim a nymph to him. Moreover, they could do so casting *upstream*.

This was an important point, because many of the dry-fly purists regarded downstream nymph fishing as little more than worming, for it is possible to cast a nymph across a stream and let the current drift it down, past the noses of dozens of fish. The fisherman is thereby hoping that some fish will take the fly at some point in its drift. This method therefore relied more on luck than skill in either casting or fly selection, and it was deemed to be less sporting. But it is effective, or can be. Someone who has the delicate feel that nymph fishing requires—the ability to detect the gentle tug that the unseen fish makes when he samples the fly—can put a great many fish in the net. (A riverkeeper on the Test told me not long ago that a good downstream nymph fisherman could clean out a section of the river, so effective is the technique. There are, therefore, practical aspects to the debate.)

It is possible, as the Jacobins said, to fish a nymph to a particular, known fish, and the trick is knowing when to strike, since you may not always feel the tug. The reason here is that you are fishing upstream (to avoid being seen), throwing the fly above the target fish, and letting it swim down to him. That means the line will have some slack in it, and the angler will therefore have to watch for the strike, even though he probably cannot see the submerged fly. It isn't easy, and therefore could be considered "sporting" as far as the English clubs were concerned. If you detect inconsistencies and elements of illogic in this debate, that is because they are there.

This dry-versus-wet-fly debate still goes on. There is no answer, of course. It is merely a matter of preference, and most fly fishermen are not purists—they will use whatever fly seems necessary, given the conditions. As in many other areas of life, we in the United States are less constrained by the forms of sport than are our counterparts in England. But there seems to be a general agreement that, all things being equal in terms of the odds of catching trout, it's more enjoyable to catch them on a dry fly because you can see the fish come to the surface to slash at or sip in the fly, and you have to set the hook while watching the action unfold—a job that your excitement makes more difficult than it should be. And it all takes place in a split second.

In short, dry-fly fishing is generally more exciting, more fun. But that is not to say that the other forms are inherently inferior or that they are not satisfying, too. It's just that there is something special about floating a dry fly over a fish that you know is feeding, seeing the fish take the fly (perhaps after several, or more, offerings), setting the hook, and then landing the fish. The element of luck is minimized; the need for skill in fly selection and presentation is at a premium. And there is a satisfying structure to the process, a beginning (spotting the rising fish), a middle (selecting the right fly), and an end (presenting the fly and hooking the fish).

That's why a lot of people prefer dry-fly fishing.

Also, there are times when a dry fly is the most effective kind, such as during a hatch. But there are other times when fish are not feeding on the surface anywhere. At those times fishing a dry fly probably is a waste of time. It would be far better to try a nymph or streamer. The conditions should dictate the choice of fly.

One final point about the dry-fly debate: it underscores one of the most gratifying elements of fly fishing—no one knows all the answers. As Izaak Walton pointed out three centuries ago: "Angling may be said to be so like the mathematics that it can never be fully learnt." There is always something to think about and discuss, even argue about. And there is no right answer in most of these debates, which means that everyone can emerge from a discussion with the satisfying certainty that one's opponent is badly informed, or worse. There is so much information to assimilate about fly fishing, there are so many theories to wade through, that a person could spend his life simply studying the subject and never fishing at all. Or a person could simply fish and never give these various debates a second thought. As with dry flies and nymphs, it's largely a matter of preference.

FLY ELEMENTS

People who studied classical philosophy in school will no doubt remember this famous syllogism:

> All fly fishermen are anglers.
> Socrates is a fly fisherman.
> Therefore, Socrates is an angler.

That may not be precisely the way it went in the original Greek, but the point is that fly fishermen share the designation "angler" with their brothers of the worm and spoon. The word "angler" stems from "angle," which stems from the Anglo Saxon word "angel," meaning hook. Modern anglers could therefore refer to themselves as hookers, but probably the term will not become popular. "Anglers" is better, anyway, because it is important to preserve tradition. Note, too, that the Angles who invaded Britain took their name from a place called Angul, a hook-shaped district in Holstein. So it is only appropriate that the Anglish, or English, should have such an important role in the evolution of the sport.

The hook is the common denominator of angling. It is also the building block of the fly, the only essential part. Have trout ever struck at a bare hook? Unquestionably, and in so doing they created the ultimate minimalist fly. So it seems that trout flies do not necessarily need elaborate dressings, but no fly can be successful without a hook.

Having said that, what else is there to know about a hook? Only a few things. First, hooks bear watching. They are made of wire, and many trout flies are tied on hooks which you can bend between two fingers. The smaller the hook, the more delicate the wire. Over time, they can lose their original shape. Anglers sometimes throw their flies into bushes or snag them on logs in the stream, and in pulling a fly free they can bend the hook. Trout will also bend a hook as they fight to get free of it. Big fish can straighten a hook. It's wise to check your hook periodically to make sure that it has retained its original shape.

Hooks also become dull with use, either because of rust or because they've bounced off boulders too many times or stuck in too many tree limbs. A dull hook can result in lost fish, because the hook does not penetrate the fish's jaw sufficiently. If you run into a series of hook-ups and quick losses, check the sharpness of your hook. One way to tell if the hook is sharp enough is to drag it down your thumbnail. If it sticks in, it's likely sharp enough. Don't push too hard, though. A pocket-size hook hone is a good investment.

A hook also has a barb. Many fly fishermen like to fish with barbless flies, and it's a relatively simple matter to use needle-nosed pliers or a hemostat to flatten the barb. There are two very good reasons to do this. First, it makes it easier to get the hook out of the fish's mouth once you've landed him. Most people agree that fishing barbless does not cause you to lose more fish. If you play a fish

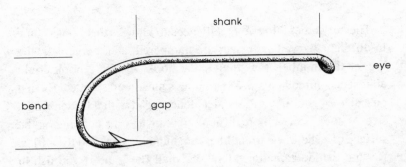

shank

eye

bend

gap

ANATOMY OF A HOOK

properly, keeping the line tight, he will stay on. Once you land the fish, you can easily remove a barbless hook, and it does little damage to the fish's mouth. Most fly fishermen release rather than keep their trout, and the faster you release a fish, the less stressful the whole adventure is for him. He can return to the water with a minimum of injury to his mouth and a minimum of time spent gasping in the alien air. Sometimes a fish will take the fly deeper in his mouth than either you or he would prefer. In such a case, having a barbless hook makes extraction a great deal easier.

The second good reason to fish barbless hooks is that it's easier to remove them from the seat of your pants, back of your hat, or, worse yet, your own ears or fingers. Self-hooking happens. But we can minimize the embarrassment and discomfort if we're able to extract the hook as efficiently as we inserted it. What's more, anglers often fish with friends, and it is deeply mortifying to hook them, especially since they generally refuse to run or jump about as a trout might, and instead restrict themselves to observations about your lineage. Not infrequently, they will overreact and, perhaps, blaspheme. The faster these hooks are removed, the faster the feast of reason and flow of soul will return to the stream or the boat.

The long part of the hook is called the shank. The distance between the shank and the point of the hook is called the gap. Then there's the point and the barb and the eye, into which you try to insert the leader. Unless and until a person wants to get into tying flies, chances are that's as much hook terminology as he will need.

The only other thing you really need to know is that hooks come in different sizes. These sizes are numbered, and, perversely, the bigger the number, the smaller the hook. A size 2 hook could almost accommodate one of grandma's meat loafs, while a fly tied on a size 24 is difficult to see, let alone thread with a leader. And a size 24 hook is even more difficult to see when it's bobbing on the surface of a shallow current line, caught in the glare and the riffles. But big fish do sometimes feed on small flies, and if you fish in productive waters you will one day catch a twenty-four-inch fish on a size 24 fly. Note that the hook size determines the size of the fly. Most experienced anglers refer not only to the artificial flies but also to the actual insects by these same sizes.

Most fly fishing for trout (again a huge generalization) is done with flies ranging from sizes 8 through 24, though some big ugly streamer patterns designed to catch really big trout are tied on larger hooks. Further, most respectable trout—say twelve inches and up—are taken on flies ranging from size 10 to size 20, I would bet.

Probably the best way to describe the other elements of a fly would be to concentrate on a dry fly, which has the most complicated design. If you understand the terminology of the dry fly, you will understand all the others—wet, nymph, streamer, and so on.

The first thing you'll probably notice about a dry fly is the hackle. You have seen pictures of Queen Elizabeth I and of Walter Raleigh and various other dandies of the Elizabethan Age. Invariably, they will be wearing stiff lace collars that stick out several inches all around their necks. These collars look uncomfortable, but fashion will have its way. The stiff white ruffs are like the hackle on a dry fly—a circular collar around the neck of the fly, just below the eye of the hook, that sticks out at a right angle to the hook's shank. The Elizabethan ruff served no functional purpose, but the hackle on a dry fly is not merely decorative. It's basic purpose is to keep the fly resting high and reasonably dry on the surface of the water.

This hackle is not made of lace or cloth, but of hackle! You've heard the expression "That raised his hackles," another way of saying someone got angry and aggressive. The term comes from the collar of stiff feathers around a rooster's neck. When he's annoyed, the rooster's hackles stand out from his neck. They probably serve to make him look bigger and more menacing to a rival, and they may offer some protection to his throat. Individual hackle feathers have stiff barbs all along the stem. That is, each "hair" (technically, "barb") of a rooster-neck feather is itself stiff, unlike, say, the corresponding barbs of body feathers, which are very soft. A fly tier will take one of these hackle feathers, tie it to a hook, and then wind it around the hook in a way that lets the individual barbs of the feather stand out at a right angle to the shank of the hook. The result is a ruff collar that will support the rest of the fly, hold the body above the surface of the water, and allow it to float longer distances. The roosters in question are raised for the purpose of growing fine hackles. If you go into a fly shop that specializes in fly-tying materials, you'll see dozens of different types of "necks" in different colors and patterns (speckled, for example). These are the rooster-neck skins from which the fly tier can pluck hundreds of hackle feathers. Different fly patterns call for different types or colors of hackle. Since most fly patterns require only one hackle feather, one neck goes a long way.

Sometimes the hackle on a fly is *not* tied to resemble a ruff. Instead, it's spiraled around the hook so that ultimately it covers the entire length of the shank. The fly then resembles the brushy end of a gun-cleaning rod. This technique is called palmering. Nowadays, flies with palmered hackles are less common than those with hackle collars.

The hackle fibers stick out only a fraction of an inch, and a fly tier needs to select each individual hackle feather carefully, because the length of the barbs that stand perpendicular to the hook shaft should not, as a rule, exceed some fraction of the length of the hook shank. Here again, though, there are many variations, and some fly patterns call for hackle of an exaggerated length.

Each hackle fiber (barb) is water-resistant. Hackle barbs don't get waterlogged easily. Further, because the individual barbs are relatively stiff, they can support the rest of the fly on the surface tension. Some of the individual fibers, though, will penetrate the surface tension even as the mass of barbs holds the fly above the surface. People who have studied the action of flies from the fish's perspective have said that, from below, most of the surface looks like a mirror and these hackle barbs break through this mirror and look like tiny flashes of light. We can assume, therefore, that they attract the trout's eye.

Since a primary purpose of hackle is to keep s fly resting on the surface, you might surmise that it's used on dry flies. But most wet patterns also have hackle. Some use what's known as soft hackles; as a wet fly with a soft hackle swims through the water, the waving motion attracts the eye of the trout.

Now let's look at the body of the fly. Body materials also vary, as you would expect, but you'll hear a great deal about "dubbing." Many fly bodies are made of dubbing. This is made from animal fur, such as muskrat or rabbit. The fly tier will take a pinch of this fur, rub it between two fingers, and spin it around some thread, thereby creating a strand that looks very much like yarn. He will then wind this furry thread around the shank of the hook. Both the material and the technique of spinning it around the hook shank are called dubbing.

Some bodies are not made of fur, but rather of feathers. A luminescent green strand from a peacock's tail, called herl, can be wound around the shank of a hook to form the body of the fly. The possibilities for body materials, in other words, are vast. The object, of course, is to design a fly that either resembles some specific aquatic insect or resembles nothing at all and merely attracts a trout's curiosity. Those two broad guidelines allow for an infinite number of fly designs. Whether they work or not is another question.

Then there's a tail. The tail, like the hackles, is designed to support a dry fly on the water, as well as to create a moderately realistic appearance. Tails are constructed out of a few or a couple of hackle barbs.

Not all dry flies have wings. In fact, one theorist opined that the hackle itself looked like wings in motion to a trout, and that additional wings are therefore superfluous. Whether that's true is another of those unanswerable questions which give rise to so much satisfying debate. But the fact is most dry flies have not only hackle but also wings. These wings are attached in front of the body, and are generally made from small feathers or hair (elk hair, for example), varying in color according to the actual fly which the artificial is intended to imitate. Thus, the all-purpose Adams mayfly imitation has two barred feathers tied to stand straight up to imitate the silhouette of a mayfly dun, while a common caddis pattern uses elk hair tied flat over the body to imitate the down-wing silhouette of a caddisfly.

That's about it for a dry fly—hackle, body, tail, wings. Wet flies, nymphs, and streamers have many of the same elements. All will have some body materials; many will have hackles (soft hackles to attract attention as the fly moves through the water, for example); some may have wings. The variations are endless, and every serious fly tier has at least one theory about what makes an effective design.

The same basic elements apply to terrestrials. Ants, for example, are essentially all body—a few scraps of fuzz tied around the middle with some thread to create the two-part body that all picnickers are familiar with. Grasshoppers can be more elaborate, and some tiers even put legs on them in an attempt to create something that looks exactly like its real-life counterpart. Other tiers believe that verisimilitude is not the object and that trout cannot see the top of a grasshopper, only the underside which is in contact with the water. Having an anatomically correct fly, they say, is therefore not necessary and is a waste of fly-tying time. The subject is yet another opportunity for debate and controversy.

Flies designed to work below the surface may incorporate some lead or other heavy material somewhere in the design. Not surprisingly, these are called weighted flies. Lead wire may be wrapped around the hook shank so the fly will sink immediately and work along the bed of a stream to imitate a drifting nymph or other denizen of the bottom. A small metal bead slipped onto the hook provides weight and a bit of glitter. Occasionally, an angler will attach small lead shot to the leader just above the fly so that it sinks rapidly even though the fly itself is not weighted. This approach is often a last-ditch tactic reserved for slow days, because it makes casting a lot more difficult (in fact, the technique is called "chuck and duck") and greatly improves the odds of self-hooking, since the normal action of fly line, leader, and fly are all altered by the weight of the lead shot. Much the same sort of thing happens when casting a weighted fly, but there is something about that piece of lead shot attached a few inches above an unweighted fly that makes this form of casting, for me at least, difficult and joyless. But every now and then it is, like paying bills, a necessary evil.

WHETHER TO MATCH THE HATCH: THAT IS THE QUESTION

The great "match the hatch" question has a couple of facets. The first involves a straightforward and sensible proposition—a fly fisherman should try to offer the trout a fly that looks like the natural flies the trout is already eating. When a hatch of mayflies is in process, and the surface is bestrewn with floating duns of a particular mayfly species, trout rise to the surface and take the flies. And since in most cases (though not always) only one particular species will be hatching at a time, the trout will concentrate on that insect and will probably ignore every other form of food in the stream. There is little sense in casting a stonefly imitation when the trout are feeding greedily on a mayfly. The angler should therefore "match the hatch," which simply amounts to selling what the customers are buying.

There's nothing in that theory that any sensible person could disagree with, and yet the idea of matching the hatch has created some controversy—chiefly, I think, because of the implication that the angler must be able to recognize exactly what is hatching. This further implies that an angler must become an accomplished amateur entomologist. And, in fact, many fly fishermen are exactly that. They can tell you the Latin names of the various bugs that come off the stream and identify them in their various stages of metamorphosis: nymph, dun, and spinner. This sort of detailed knowledge can be intimidating to someone whose memories of science class chiefly involve hopeless toil followed inevitably by disappointing grades, tearful mothers, and stern fathers. (In my own case, I remember that entomology is the study of insects because the word starts with "ent," which resembles "ant." That also makes it easy to remember that etymology is the study of the origin of words, because it is not the study of bugs. Simple.)

While many people find detailed entomological knowledge and study intensely satisfying, that degree of scientific effort is not necessary. An angler who has no interest in the science of the sport, whose only knowledge of Latin is a dimly remembered phrase from high school (*"America est pulchra"*), can still enjoy the sport and be successful even when standing in the stream during a hatch of insects whose English names he does not know, much less their scientific names. While it is true that the fly you offer rising fish should resemble the fly they are eating, the key is in the fly's appearance and behavior rather than its identity. And appearance means *size and color and design*, while behavior means both the *presentation* of the fly (getting it in the trout's vicinity with a minimum of disturbance) and its *action* once on the water.

At the risk of stating the stunningly obvious, trout react to what they see. The effectiveness of a fly, therefore, is a matter of appearance. If you can duplicate the appearance and motion of the natural flies that trout are taking, you have a good chance of catching fish, regardless of your scientific expertise. In sum, the great match-the-hatch question closely resembles the great dry-fly debate: sensible ideas that evolved into extreme quasi-theological positions as a result of zealotry. There's nothing wrong with either approach, but all anglers do not have to adopt the orthodoxy in order to have a good time fly fishing.

There are other opinions on matching the hatch. As in the stock market, there are the contrarians. Their approach is based on the fact that a major hatch brings with it one significant difficulty—too many natural flies on the water. If you've selected a fly that matches the hatch and manage to float it past the trout in a way that duplicates the natural action of a real fly caught in the current, how do you differentiate your fly from all the others? It's simply one more debutante in a frilly dress, indistinguishable from the rest of the cotillion. You've done everything properly, yet your offering is ignored because of the trout's embarrassment of riches. To change the metaphor, when you go to the ballpark and order a hot dog, you don't select an individual wiener. They all look alike, taste alike, and give the same heartburn. The only selection involves the species—the hot dog. Same with the trout during a hatch. (Of course, you would reject a wiener that was poorly presented—say, dropped on the floor before being offered to you. But all presentations being equal, one wiener is much like another.) The contrarian approach argues that in a hatch of hot dogs, you are more likely to notice a bratwurst. So why not offer something that catches the trout's eye because it's unique? The contrarian says that during a major hatch it is sometimes more effective to use an attractor—something that not only does not match the current hatch but doesn't even match any real insect. Sometimes this theory works. Sometimes.

The difficulty with the contrarian view is that trout are often extremely "selective." That word encapsulates much of the frustration of trout fishing. When trout are feeding on one species of insect, they tend to concentrate on that one type and ignore other offerings regardless of how appealing their sponsor might think they are. Entire books and many articles have been written about selective trout, and when the are selectively feeding on a particular insect, an angler might as well give up all other theories and offer the appropriate imitation, if he can figure out just what it is. That's not always so easy, because during a hatch the trout might be feeding on emergers just below the surface and ignoring the fully hatched duns. The trout are making surface disturbances, and these may create the impression that they're taking the duns, when in fact they're ignoring them. An angler eager to match the hatch ties on a dun and then casts away in ever-mounting mystification and frustration. Matching the hatch offers no guarantees.

Anyway, the basic conclusion we can draw from the match-the-hatch debate is that as a general rule it's a good general rule. It's just not necessary to digest the details of an entomology text in order to be successful. The important thing is to look at the water, see the insects the trout are taking, and then present something that looks like that bug. And the key phrase is "looks like."

So, if the object is to select the right fly based on observation of the naturals, the question then becomes: What are we looking for and what are the criteria for selection? What makes the right fly? As I mentioned before, there are two basic answers—appearance and behavior—and each of those answers has a couple of components. For appearance there is color, size, and design, not necessarily in that order. For behavior there is presentation and motion. The common denominator in all of these components is the vision of the trout, since in all cases we are concerned with creating the appropriate appearance. Before we can intelligently discuss what a fly should look and act like, we have to understand how a trout sees, and the effect its vision has on the trout's behavior. And we need to look at two aspects of the trout's vision: how it sees the surface of the stream when it's looking for floating flies, and how it sees everything else beneath the surface.

THE CONE

Trout have a restrictive cone of vision. The cone is caused by what happens to light as it penetrates the surface of the water. When a light ray hits the surface, the ray bends. It refracts. I believe it was in physics class that we learned about refraction; I wondered about the usefulness of this information at the time, but now I understand. It is directly relevant to trout fishing, because trout, like people, need light in order to see. But the trout's light must first pass through the surface of the stream. The angle of the light also affects the fish's vision, because low-angle light simply bounces off the surface instead of penetrating it, and in so doing creates glare both above and below the surface. Neither the angler above nor the trout below can see through this glare; it seems like a mirror to both.

Light coming in from a slightly higher angle does penetrate the surface, but it is still subject to refraction. The result is that trout see things rather differently than do humans. Trout look up at the surface of the stream and see only a circular window. They can see anything resting on that window and they can see beyond the window—through it—to the sky above, trees, the bank, and an angler standing nearby wondering which fly to use. Outside that circular window, the surface is nothing but glare, a mirror on which and through which the fish can't see anything. It's as though they are constantly looking through a camera lens (literally, I suppose, a fish-eye lens). The farther they are from the surface, the greater the size of the circular panorama; the closer they are to the surface, the smaller their field of surface vision.

Or think of it this way. The trout is wearing an inverted dunce cap. The point is resting on top of his head; the open end is on the surface of the stream. The deeper he is in the water, the greater the diameter of the open end of the cap. The closer he is to the surface, the smaller the diameter of the circular opening. Anything on the surface that is outside that circle is invisible to the trout; anything within that circle the trout can see. This opening is traditionally called the "window," and the obvious implication for a fly fisherman is that a fly must float into the trout's window in order to be seen and eaten. For all practical purposes, anything that floats outside the window does not exist.

If the trout's window is smaller the closer he is to the surface, and if, when the trout is feeding on surface flies, he is lying close to the surface (which he does to conserve energy), then it follows that an artificial fly must float very close to the fish in order to be visible. The angler can't expect the trout to chase a fly that falls outside the window. It's not that the fish is lazy; he just doesn't see the fly.

More bad news about refraction. Not only does the angler have to float a fly into the fish's surface field of vision, but he must be aware that refraction widens the fish's ability to see things *above* the surface of the water. The circumference of the dunce cap stops at the surface. From there the bent light rays flatten and shoot outward—as though the dunce cap has a flat brim all around it. Think of it as the reverse of the refraction phenomenon, so that above the surface the fish's view is expanded, and he can easily detect a hopeful angler peering over the bank in search of quarry. For that reason, people who fish chalk streams, where the surface of the water is calm and therefore the optics of the trout are unobstructed, will often stalk a fish on hands and knees in order to stay below the fish's field of vision above the surface. In freestone streams, the need for stealth is less pressing, because the ripples on the surface distort the fish's view, like raindrops on a camera lens.

The cone of vision applies only to things on the surface and above. The fish's view of his subsurface colleagues and menu items is not materially affected by refracted light, and his vision is restricted only by the clarity of the water, the amount of light available, and the trout's anatomy (the position of its eyes determines the edge of its peripheral vision).

THE COLOR OF A FLY

Artists have long been attracted to the American Southwest and the south of France because of the quality of the light and its effect on color. To put it differently, light is essential to the eye's ability to detect color. The brighter the light, the more intense is the color. Trout can see color, and yet they don't generally like strong light. As Datus Proper points out in his book *What the Trout Said*, trout can't squint. Most experienced anglers believe that larger trout are reluctant to feed when the light is intense, and this is supported by the experience of many fishing guides who look upon overcast days as an opportunity to catch big, wary browns.

Trout apparently see objects, including flies, more clearly when the light is lower, but their ability to see color diminishes as the light fades. The implication is that the color of a fly is important in bright light, but less so when the light fades. That makes sense, because to a human eye the colors of the woods or the mountains are rich and varied at noon but monochromatic at night. And yet, if trout are reluctant to feed in bright light, is their increased ability to see color important to the angler? Does color really stimulate a trout to take a fly? As the King of Siam observed, "It's a puzzlement." Or, we can fall back on the all-purpose answer to any thorny fly-fishing question: "It depends."

Certainly it is true that natural insects do have different colors. And since trout are indisputably selective at times, it follows that the color of the fly they are eating has some impact on their ability to recognize the fly they want to the exclusion of all others.

All of this implies that the best course of action during a hatch is to try to match the color of the fly to the color of the naturals, but not to get overwrought about a perfect match. That would appear to be especially true on overcast days when the trout may be more active, but when their ability to distinguish minor variations in color is reduced.

One example of the use of color is the female spinner, a mayfly in the process of depositing her eggs. These mayflies have yellow egg sacks on the underside of their abdomens. When spinners are on the stream depositing their eggs, an imitation that includes the color denoting the egg sack may pay dividends to the angler. Are trout attracted to the yellow egg sack or are they just eating the spinners? Does the yellow egg sack indicate additional nutritive value? *¿Quien sabe?*

Bear in mind that the discussion of color so far has dealt only with dry flies. The problem of the trout's window applies only to flies on the surface. Wet flies, nymphs, and streamers, all of which work below the surface, are readily visible to the trout. Color is therefore likely to be an important element in the fly's attractiveness. Stream conditions (such as murky water after a rainstorm or flood) as well as the availability of light from above affect the trout's ability to see sunken flies. Theories abound concerning color in these conditions. Some say it's best to use a brightly colored fly in order to attract the trout's attention in the gloomy depths. Others recommend dark flies for dark water. When in doubt, probably the best course of action is to try to match the color of your fly to the natural colors of the creature you're imitating—whether it's a fly or sculpin or dace or scud or whatever. When that doesn't work, try something else.

It's worth noting that most attractors are distinguished primarily by their colors, rather than their shapes. For example, a Royal Wulff has a silhouette that suggests a mayfly, but its combination of colors is different from anything natural. This implies, to me at least, that color can be an important factor in attracting trout. Moreover, the primary thing that differentiates one classic salmon fly from another (and salmon are close relatives of trout) is color.

Finally, in periods of desperation, fishing guides will often put on a big, ugly wet fly tied with sparkling materials. To me those sparkles are nothing more than intensified color, since color, after all, is a product of light. Why bother with the sparkles if color is not a key?

The color of trout flies is like advertising: everyone agrees that it has an impact, but no one is sure exactly how large the impact is or how that impact compares to other factors affecting consumer behavior. But clearly, when a hatch is in progress, one of the elements you need to match is the color of the naturals. Almost everyone would agree with that, except, perhaps, the odd contrarian.

THE DESIGN OF A FLY

It's sad, perhaps, but true that some fly fishermen occasionally go to a bar at the end of an angling day. (Walton himself extolled the virtues of "an honest ale-house where we shall find a cleanly room, lavender in the windows and twenty ballads stuck about the wall.") And though a Carrie Nation might disapprove, these nocturnal wanderings off the straight and narrow do have some benefits. While refreshing themselves, many anglers have no doubt noticed the sparkling sphere that hangs above a typical roadhouse dance floor. A spotlight shining on the rotating ball throws off shafts of light that enhance the appearance of the dancers (for whom, in many cases, normal light would be unwelcome). These shafts of light often have a prismatic effect and create various colors.

Having noticed this phenomenon myself, once, it occurred to me that it was a good explanation of the "light-pattern" effect a fly has as it approaches the trout's "window."

Here's what happens to a dry fly that lands upstream from the trout's window of vision (once again, Datus Proper's *What the Trout Said* is the source; though these aren't Mr. Proper's words):

The fly lands in the area that, from the trout's perspective, is a mirror of glare created by light rays that glance off the surface of the water beyond the trout's window.

The fly floats downstream toward the window.

When the fly approaches the window, but before it gets there, the trout notices the hackle points and probably the hook and tail—all of which are penetrating the surface tension and therefore breaking through the mirror of glare. These points look like pinpoints of light. The body of the fly may also become gradually visible—assuming it penetrates the surface tension. The stiffer the hackles and tail, the less of the body in the tension. But the color of the body—however much breaks through the surface—will be clearly visible.

The fly's wings—assuming it has any—now become visible, because of the refraction of the light rays above the surface of the water. (Remember the reverse effect of refraction from the trout's perspective—above the surface. This is the brim on the dunce cap.) In other words, assuming the fly is a mayfly dun with upright wings, the wings are above the surface and will come into view "before they should" because of the action of refraction.

Just before the fly breaks into the edge of the window, the pinpoints of light intensify and create an effect similar to the roadhouse light sphere—sparkles and colors of the full range of the spectrum. The actual color of the fly is washed out by this display, just as the actual colors of the dancers are muted by the rotating light of the sphere.

The fly then breaks into the window and the effect of refraction disappears as does the light display, and the actual appearance of the fly, for better or worse, becomes clear.

At this point, the trout decides to take it or reject it—assuming he hasn't already decided to ignore it because, while it was an interesting light show, the fly proved itself to be fraudulent before it got to the window since it was acting unnaturally (for example, moving slower or faster than the current would dictate, or moving sideways to the current; more on this later).

Aside from offering some good opportunities for conversation with casual acquaintances at a roadhouse, what is the value of this information? First, it indicates the value of getting a good float— that is, casting the fly so it drops upstream of the trout and then floats naturally in the current down toward the trout's window. This, of course, implies that you can see the trout in the first place (here again is the chalk-stream, dry-fly purist's argument). But even if you're casting to a spot where trout should be (a good feeding lie), you still need to drop the fly above the suspected lie and then let it float naturally into the area where you suspect the trout to be. *How* you do that is a matter of technique. *That* you should do it is a function of the way a trout sees. The trout, in other words, is accustomed to seeing this light show followed by the appearance of the fly. He knows how the whole drama should play out.

Second, it shows that different fly designs will have different effects on what the trout sees. High-riding dry flies—well supported by hackles, well dosed with floatant, and sporting effective tails—will probably put on a more spectacular light show than low-riding flies whose bodies are submerged in the surface tension. The main lesson from this information is, I suppose, if you're fishing dry flies, make sure that they float well. Further, as Datus Proper notes, trout seem to be somewhat less selective about really high-floating dry flies. Perhaps this is because of the attractiveness of the light show or because they can't see them quite as clearly, or both.

Other dry patterns, intentionally, have no hackles and are designed to ride low in the water. This means the light show is probably less spectacular but the color is more visible. Does that mean that color is a more important factor with low-riding flies? Maybe so.

Again, all of this applies to dry-fly fishing. Wet flies of all varieties are not affected by the light-show effect, because they don't float on the surface of the stream.

The other factor to consider in the design or shape of flies is size. There are two things to think about here. First, there is the venerable notion that anglers should use big flies for big fish. This is common sense of a sort, because trout do use some energy in eating, and they want the maximum return for their investment. But even relatively big fish will occasionally feed selectively on very small flies. Matching the hatch, therefore, means matching the size as well as the pattern of the fly. Then, too, really big trout (say, over five pounds) seldom feed on the surface, and so for those big ones we have to use wet flies that are both big and attractive—streamers and large nymphs. With nymphs, since the actual insect is largely undifferentiated by species (they all look pretty much alike) and since they come in a narrow range of neutral colors, selectivity is not nearly as big a problem as it is with dry flies. Something big and juicy-looking should do the trick if it behaves normally, drifting along the bottom in a way that suggests normal nymph behavior. Nymph fishermen, in other words, don't seem to spend as much time agonizing over fly selection. Perhaps this is another reason why the dry-fly purists regard them with some suspicion.

The problem of matching the hatch comes down to noticing what's on the water and selecting something from your fly box that represents the same approximate species, in the same approximate color and size as the fly the trout are currently eating. One more factor may be obvious but should be mentioned. That is, the angler should also match the *stage* of the fly. For example, if the trout are taking mayfly duns, it probably will not be effective to offer them a spinner pattern, even though the spinner is of the same size and color. Spinner patterns are tied with their wings out straight to imitate dead and dying mayflies that have just mated, deposited their eggs, and fallen, disheveled and spread-eagled, to the surface. Duns, on the other hand, have upright wings and are ready to fly off to their next metamorphosis (into a spinner) and their subsequent nuptials. (This premise is contradicted, admittedly, by the fact that many duns are half drowned and disheveled on the surface; a new hatch does not uniformly resemble a sailing regatta.) But as a general rule, when trout are eating spinners, give them a spinner of the same size and color. When they're eating duns, give them a dun of the same size and color. If you present the fly properly and manage to float it naturally to a feeding fish (or to a likely feeding lie), you may get your reward.

In addition to the appearance of the fly, another important factor is its behavior, and that leads to the subject of technique. But technique is a means to an end, a way of synchronizing the angler to the ways of the trout. So, technique needs to be understood in the context of the third great factor in the art of fly fishing (after water and food). And that factor is trout behavior.

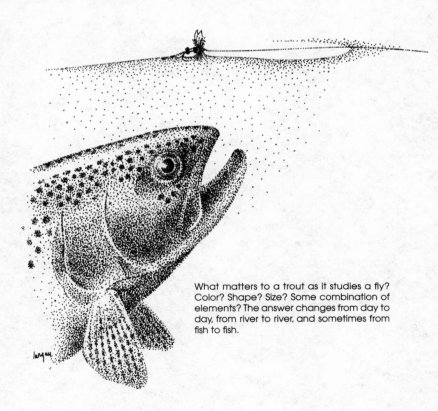

What matters to a trout as it studies a fly? Color? Shape? Size? Some combination of elements? The answer changes from day to day, from river to river, and sometimes from fish to fish.

CHAPTER 5

Trout Behavior

This is the excellent foppery of the world, that, when we are sick in fortune—often the surfeit of our own behavior—we make guilty of our disasters the sun, the moon, and the stars; as if we were villains by necessity, fools by heavenly compulsion, knaves, thieves and treachers by spherical predominance, drunkards, liars and adulterers by an enforced obedience of planetary influence.

—Shakespeare, *King Lear*
act 1, scene 2

I GUESS THAT MEANS SHAKESPEARE DIDN'T BELIEVE in the Solunar Tables, at least when it comes to people. But it's fair to say that trout, unlike humans, are predominantly "fools by heavenly compulsion." Their behavior is a response to conditions, not a matter of choice. And those conditions include "the sun, the moon and the stars." We know, for example, that bright sunlight dampens their enthusiasm for the angling game. As for the moon and stars, it's generally believed that sea-run trout and salmon find their way across oceans and back to their spawning grounds by celestial navigation. Once close to their natal stream, they use their sense of smell. Their migration and return is a phenomenon that, when you consider it, is nothing short of sublime, especially when you remember that their view of the sun and stars is distorted by light refraction. How do they know how to adjust their calculations?

Weather affects trout, too, even wind, though why a creature that lives underwater should notice the wind perplexes most people.

("When the wind is east, the fishing is least," goes the saying in England, and I have yet to talk to a professional guide in either fishing or hunting who does not lose the edge off his optimism when an east wind is blowing.) And a falling barometer will turn trout sullen and uninterested in playing their part. While they often appear willful, in reality trout are more acted upon than actors— "more sinned against than sinning," to reprise King Lear.

Besides the external factors that act on them, trout are subject to genetic programs—call them instincts—that force them to do certain things at certain times, most notably reproduce. Like their partners, the mayflies, they are at certain times prisoners of a sexual urge, while the rest of the time they are prisoners of their other needs and of external forces.

With that sort of deterministic view of these creatures, you'd think it would be easy to catch them. But, of course, their primary urge is for survival, and that's what makes them difficult. Like all creatures that live and sometimes die by hunting, they are wary and alert.

We know what they need—food, a livable environment (good water quality, not too much current), safety from predators, and, once a year or so, a spouse. The question then becomes: How do these needs affect their behavior? We know their motives, but how do those motives translate into action?

Before attempting to answer that question, perhaps we should ask what, precisely, we're talking about when we speak of "trout." Who are these creatures whose behavior we want to understand in order to catch them?

SALMONIDS

Trout are salmonids. In other words, they are all members of the salmon family. When anglers speak of trout, they mean primarily four species: brook trout, rainbows, brown trout, and cutthroat trout. Other types of trout are sought by anglers, but these four species are the most common.

Each of the species has a certain personality, at least in the minds and lore of anglers. The brook trout is generally regarded as a beautiful but somewhat dimwitted creature. This perception may derive not so much from the brook trout's lack of mental ability, but rather from its lack of wariness compared to some other trout species. That, in turn, may derive from the fact that brook trout seem to be the most aggressive of the common salmonids. In any event, brook trout seem ever willing to play the game, but they have no more patience for angling ineptitude than any other trout.

Scientists say that the brookie is not really a trout at all, but a char. This is a quibble, as far as most anglers are concerned. You can tell a brook trout because its spots are lighter than its body coloring, and this is the only trout species (along with their close cousins the lake trout) where that coloring occurs. They are often found in small streams, hence the name. In the days when people kept fish to eat, a mess of small brookies was considered a breakfast fit for a king. In some places, that is still true. They can grow large—the big brook trout of Labrador and environs are legendary, but even there we're only talking about fish in the five-pound range.

These are our Eastern native trout, the trout the pilgrims and pioneers first encountered when they left their ships. No doubt the brook trout was at least part of the answer when these early settlers asked themselves, as they must have done, why they had ever left home.

The rainbow is considered moderately intelligent. (Assigning levels of intelligence to trout, like ascribing personalities, is an exercise in anthropomorphism, but anglers do it anyway.) Acrobatic and energetic when hooked, rainbows are apt to leap and jump in fierce resentment at being stung. With a silvery body and the bright, variegated colors that give the species its common name, the rainbow is many anglers' favorite quarry. He's aggressive, a fighter.

Rainbow trout are native to the Western states, but they have been successfully transplanted to many rivers around the world. The famous chalk streams of England support rainbows in large numbers—and sizes. Some rainbows spend much of their mature life at sea, and in this they reveal their close relationship with some of the salmon family. Sea-run rainbows grow to a larger size than their freshwater colleagues, and they go by the name steelhead, a name that is not an aspersion on their intelligence but rather a reference to their predominant coloring. Steelheads, like all of the salmonid family, return to fresh water to spawn. (The word "anadromous" refers to this habit of spawning in the fresh water but running off to sea at the first opportunity, like sailors after shore leave.)

Brown trout are sometimes called German browns, and, as you would suspect, they are natives of Europe. They were successfully introduced here around the turn of the twentieth century, and they have spread throughout the United States. Browns are regarded as the wariest of the trout. They tend to lurk in shadowy places, such as along grassy stream banks that have been cut away by the current to create a shady overhang under which a fish can lie, mulling over his resentments like some misanthrope and waiting for the right morsel to float by. Strong and occasionally acrobatic, browns seem to be the most difficult to catch, and so, in the perverse logic of angling, are generally the most highly prized trout. They are dark on the top, and buttery-colored below, and spotted red and black. They are masters of the ambush. In attitude they seem to be older than the rainbows, old for their age, more serious somehow. If the rainbow is the jock with a B average, the brown is the graduate student—unsociable, businesslike, with hidden depths of menacing aggressiveness and surprising strength.

Cutthroats are native to the American West, and their name derives from two long red slashes under their jaws rather than from any tendency toward bloodthirstiness. In fact, they're generally thought to be rather mild-mannered, both in the way they tentatively, softly take the fly and in their subsequent resistance. All other things being equal, they are less highly prized (albeit only slightly) than the rainbows and browns. They sometimes—even frequently—crossbreed with rainbows, which gives scientists some difficulty about deciding what exactly a species really is. A species is generally regarded as a class of creatures that only breeds with its own kind. But, like black ducks and mallards, rainbows and cutts now and then ignore the rules of science and follow their hearts. "What's in a name?" they ask. This tendency has caused the species some difficulty, however, since wherever the cutts and rainbows reside together they tend to interbreed, and the cutthroat species seems to be the loser; that is, the rainbow characteristics seem to dominate. Largely for this reason, cutthroats have not been successfully transplanted from Western waters, and they are busy trying to hold their own in the West—not against predation or pollution so much as against the siren call of the rainbows. The offspring of these unions are fertile, unlike the offspring of some other interbreeding species.

In the salmonid family there are three genera, and within each genus are the various species of trout and salmon. The following chart summarizes all of that, and I include it only to show the interesting relationships among these various fish. The rainbow, for example, is a closer relative of the Pacific salmon than of the brown trout. The criteria for these classifications have been developed by biologists and have to do mainly with things such jaw structure and number of scales and other such details that most anglers cheerfully ignore.

Salmonids

I. Genus *Onchorynchus*
  A. Pacific Salmon
    1.) Chinook
    2.) Coho
    3.) Sockeye
    4.) Pink
    5.) Chum
  B. Rainbow Trout
  C. Cutthroat Trout

II. Genus *Salmo*
  A. Atlantic Salmon
  B. Brown Trout

III. Genus *Salvelinus* (Char)
  A. Brook Trout
  B. Lake Trout

Behavioral Characteristics

Although there are some slight behavioral variations among the species, the important characteristics are shared by all the trout—brookies, rainbows, browns, cutthroats, and so on. From the angler's viewpoint, the really important characteristics are those that relate to the question of how to catch these fish.

We know that trout in rivers and streams—moving water—are territorial, and we know why: they rely on the current to deliver food to them in a predictable and efficient manner. Trout living in lakes, of course, cannot afford to be territorial, because living in still water is like living in a cheap hotel—when they call down for room service, no one answers, so they must go out and get their own meals.

Each trout in a stream stakes out his own territory. The territory includes a feeding station, or lie, and a holding station, or lie. The bigger the fish, the bigger his territory will be. Trout seem to have a keen sense of personal space, and will defend it against intruders. The bigger the fish, the more space he seems to need to be comfortable. His need for more space may also have to do with a larger fish's need for more food, since it seems logical to assume that a larger territory will have a greater total volume of food drifting through it.

A second factor affecting territory size is the physical characteristics of the stream. A stream with a lot of rocks and boulders and therefore lots of pockets will accommodate more fish. Trout seem to be comfortable as long as they cannot see their rivals, so their territories can be smaller if the other fish are screened from view. Trout streams that have more variety in their contours and composition will, therefore, contain more fish, simply because such a stream can accommodate more territories (assuming that the stream offers sufficient food for all).

Scientists have discovered that when a trout has taken up a position in his territory—perhaps just under the surface in order to take mayfly duns—he will move up to take a fly and then return to the exact spot he just left—within a fraction of an inch. He may move off to take a submerged fly or nymph, but will again return to the same holding spot. The trout puts his nose in the current and stays right there, while the rest of his body undulates easily against the current. From above, these fish look exactly like the waving, trailing weeds of a chalk stream. Is this habit a form of camouflage, an evolved trick of imitating a weed to fool a predator? To borrow a line from Hemingway, "Isn't it pretty to think so?"

The trout's territory will contain, in addition to a feeding lie, a holding lie—a place of refuge during periods of inactivity or alarm. So when we say that trout are territorial, it does not mean they are stationary. The feeding lie and holding lie need not be widely separated, however. In his book *Trout Biology*, Bill Willers cites a study of a nine-inch brown trout that had a territory of four square yards. In a different stream with different characteristics, that same space could accommodate a much larger fish. I mention it here to give some indication of the approximate size of trout territories. Also bear in mind that a trout may occasionally find a perfect station—a "primary lie"—that provides both food and comfortable concealment.

Trout are not particularly social. The fact that there are more than one in a particular area of a stream indicates that part of the stream is productive and comfortable, and affords sufficient cover to house a number of trout. In other words, "communities" exist as a result of conditions, not because trout are gregarious. They aren't. In fact, as we have seen, they will attack any trout that comes into their territory—as long as the invader is not too big, in which case the smaller trout will flee. The bigger fish will take the best territories and hold them as long as they remain productive and as long as an even bigger fish does not come by with an eviction notice.

WHERE ARE THEY?

Anyone who spends time in the American West and who has an interest in the history of the area must at some point think about the Indian wars of the nineteenth century. And thinking about those wars and looking at the landscapes in which they were fought always, for me at least, raises the question of how on earth the antagonists ever found each other in that endless spread of real estate. How do you locate nomads in a vast country?

Novice anglers must sometimes feel like the new lieutenant fresh from West Point who scanned the horizon and saw only empty country. A new angler looks at a stretch of water and wonders, where can they be? But we know what trout need, and if we look in the places where they can find those things, we improve the odds of finding the quarry.

Because trout are territorial, they will be where they should be. That is, an angler can look at a trout stream and identify the places where trout probably are holding. This applies primarily to freestone, runoff streams. Spring creeks lack many of the features—rocks, boulders, riffles—of runoff streams, and for that reason, spring-creek anglers rely more on spotting rising fish than on prospecting in likely spots. But in a runoff stream, spotting good lies is relatively easy. Since the trout is trying to find a spot that delivers good food, he must be close to the current lines. And since the trout wants to avoid the heavy work of holding directly in the current, there must be some protection from the flow. And finally, since the trout wants protection from predators, the lie must offer cover or depth or darkness. Trout dislike strong light both for its own sake and because it reduces their sense of security. What's more, trout are oxygen addicts. They're attracted to places where they can breathe high concentrations of dissolved oxygen: water that's cold and deep or cold and aerated. If you keep these factors in mind and take some time to examine a stretch of river or stream, you'll see a number of likely holding places:

Just behind and off to the side of a rock or boulder. Trout won't sit *directly* behind a rock, because that's dead water there— no current and therefore no food deliveries. But they will sit just inside the current that rushes around the rock. The rock gives them shelter from the flow, while they are close enough to the current to be able to grab food without much effort.

Just in front of a boulder. This may seem strange, since a trout dislikes fighting the current, but the action of the water actually creates a cushion just in front of the rock. The water bounces back upon itself. Trout like to sit in this cushion because they can easily see food drifting downstream. Since the boulder may split the current so that it runs down both sides of the rock, the trout can sit in front and take food regardless of which side of the rock it floats past. This lie seems therefore to be more productive than the lie behind and alongside the rock (which in essence only gives access to one of the current streams).

At the head or tail of a pool. A pool is a deep section of a stream. Pools in streams can often be like bottles with necks at both ends. At the head of the pool, the water is forced into a narrow chute by the bottom terrain or by rocks. This funneling of the water also funnels the food, both on and under the surface, directly to a waiting trout that might be lying just on the edge of the current line or at the end of the bottleneck where the current opens out and eases. That way, the trout can avoid the full strength of the flow and yet be close enough to intercept food easily. A similar phenomenon often occurs at the tail of the pool where water is again funneled into a narrow current. Trout wait just in front of the narrowing, and therefore have the same easy pickings as their colleagues at the head of the pool. The middle of the pool is deep and slower-moving, so it will be a likely holding lie, offering protection from predators, low light levels, cool temperatures, and easier current. And a big fish just might hang out there continuously, using it as a primary lie, assuming that the pool is large enough to support the minnows and leeches and sculpins and other favored menu items of a large trout. All in all, a pool offers most of what trout of all sizes consider essential to the good life. Not all pools feature the double bottleneck structure. Some are simply deep sections of a stream, but the principle remains—trout like the security of the depth and the predictable current lines.

Riffles and drop-offs. Large rivers accumulate gravel and small rocks and move them around in the course of regular river business. These gravel deposits build up here and there and create riffles— small, shallow rapids. When the river is low, these may be exposed islands, called gravel bars. But when the river is high, they are miniature white water. Because of the action of water against rocks, riffles are highly aerated, and fish will move into these shallows to feed and to enjoy the oxygen rush. They'll also hang out just below a riffle, where the water drops off into a deeper pool. Trout can lie in the deeper water, enjoy the safety of the depths, and still be in a position to snare food as it passes through the riffle and over the drop-off.

Waterfalls. The water flowing over the falls creates a deep pool at the base, and the action of falling water catches and holds oxygen. So, the base of a waterfall, regardless of how large, is a good place to look for trout. And, of course, the waterfall is delivering food to the fish, food caught in the turbulence and probably not in total control of its motor functions. The food that tumbles over can be easy pickings for the trout lurking there.

Grassy undercut banks. An undercut bank is like a cantilevered porch that juts out over the edge of the river. The current has carved away the space beneath the overhang, but the root system of the grass above holds the bank in place and protects it against further erosion. This is an ideal holding and feeding lie for trout, because it has everything they hold most dear: darkness, protection from predators, a current line to deliver food. Brown trout, especially, seem to like these undercuts; they suit the brown's preference for lurking in dark places. Grassy banks are also generally rich with grasshoppers that sometimes jump left instead of right and end up in the current line and the food chain almost simultaneously. (Unfortunately, grassy banks are vulnerable to cattle grazing along the river; the cows break down the banks as they eat and drink and wander around in typical bovine stupefaction. Without fences to keep the cows away from the water, good holding lies soon become muddy cattle ramps. To paraphrase Robert Frost, good fences make good fishing.)

Structure. A tree that falls into the river provides a haven for some trout. They don't lurk among the sunken branches like a bass, exactly, but they do like to lie alongside a tree trunk that's half submerged. The trunk redirects the flow of the water and also provides protection for a trout lying alongside the tree with his nose in the current waiting for food to drift by. Trout also like to lie alongside cliffs that have been worn away by eons of current. This position is similar to an undercut bank—protection above and on one side and easy access to the current line.

Current lines and drop-offs near the bank. If you stand on a bridge and watch the action of the water, you'll often see a line of foam on the surface, particularly in a bigger river. This foam line is caused by the action of the water. It tells you exactly where the current is, and you already know that trout will be near the current, so floating a fly in the foam line is generally a good idea. Often, this line will be near shore at the point where the water starts to get deep. Trout like to be there because the depth provides protection while the current provides food.

Under overhanging branches. Trees hanging over the river provide protection, or at least the illusion of protection, to a trout. Angling author Tom Rosenbauer once wrote about a trout that lived under a single-strand wire fence that stuck out over the stream. That wire made it virtually impossible for a bird of prey to attack the trout—and also made it very difficult to cast a fly to the fish. It wasn't much cover, but it was enough. It stands to reason, then, that a trout would prefer even more protection, and would therefore delight in the shade of a tree leaning out over the water and bending down so its leaves and branches are just brushing the surface in places—not so much that they change the current or intercept food, but just enough to provide shade and security.

Note that spring creeks have overhanging branches and grassy banks, too. In fact, the essence of the spring creek is a grassy bank on both sides, for the typical spring creek ambles through a meadow and carves holding places for trout along both banks as it goes. And spring creeks may have an occasional waterfall (usually manmade), as well as some of the other territorial clues that apply to freestone streams.

"NBTW." Doug Gibson, who guides on the Snake and Henrys Fork in Idaho, talks about "Nondescript brown trout water"—or NBTW. In a big river like the South Fork of the Snake, there are stretches of flat, deep-green water, often several dozen yards offshore, places that offer no particular reason (other than depth) to suspect the presence of trout. Sometimes you can drift a fly through that water, and a brown trout will rise up from those depths like a Polaris missile and grab that fly so quickly that you might be startled out of all daydreams about a rising stock market or an evening with Emmylou Harris.

Runs. Over time, a stream carves out runs, which are chutes of water deeper than the water on either side. You can tell a run because it has a different color, usually darker, than the rest of the stream. A run has swift current and may last only a few yards and may be only a foot or so wide, but it's always a good idea to float a fly through a run, since the depth and current attract and channel food, making these places attractive feeding lies for trout. The fish may sit just to one side in order to avoid the main rush of water, but they'll see anything that floats through the run.

All of these places are variations on the theme that trout are in places where they can meet their basic needs for food and safety. There are other places that meet the same criteria. And as we know, trout will sometimes be where they have no reason to be, such as in very shallow water that offers no protection but offers something else known only to the trout. Chances are that in these situations the trout's interest is temporary, and when satisfied he will return to his normal and more reasonable haunts.

All trout have similar behavior patterns, but there are regional variations. For example, conventional wisdom says that trout prefer water at about 60 to 65 degrees and that they stop feeding when water gets much colder than about 50. Yet in the San Juan River below Navajo Dam in New Mexico and in the Colorado River below Glen Canyon Dam, the water stays right around 45 degrees all year round. (Both dams release water from the lowest and coldest part of the reservoir, so the temperature stays constant.) Despite these cold temperatures, which should have the trout thinking about hibernation, the fish are very active, healthy, and aggressive feeders. The rule about generalizations comes into play again.

Speaking of dams raises another point about the presence of trout in predictable places. Sometimes Mother Nature or human nature intervenes to change things, and the results from a fishing point of view are unfortunate. Floods, obviously, will change the structure of a river and therefore change the holding lies of the resident trout. Floods can also bring silt, which not only makes breathing difficult, but also clogs up the gravel bottoms that trout need for spawning and reduces the aerating effect of water against rock. Faced with this sort of disaster, trout must move on. And dams are nothing more than manmade floods waiting to happen. When too much water is released from a dam, either accidentally or intentionally, the silt that builds up behind the dam clogs the tailwaters which up to then had been productive trout habitat, and the onrushing water scours out the holding lies and gravel and redistributes it far downstream. The trout that survive must pack up and find new lodgings. Even regular and reasonable releases from a dam will affect a trout's behavior. He may not move, but he may decide to take a siesta for the rest of the day. Trout, like many humans, like it when life follows predictable patterns.

WHAT FACTORS STIMULATE TROUT TO EAT?

This is the eternal question. There are many answers, but none that completely satisfies. For what they are worth, here are a few:

They are hungry. This is the most obvious and perhaps least useful answer, since the timing of the trout's hunger pangs is like the schedule of the subway—you know that the trains come along regularly, but you don't know exactly when, so you just have to wait. It is known that hunger is affected by the type of food the trout is eating. Large crustaceans, for example, take longer to digest than most other food, for a trout does not bother to shell his crayfish before eating them, and may suffer a post-Thanksgiving torpor after a few crawdads. Aquatic insects are more easily digested, and so, like Chinese food, linger longer in the memory than in the digestive tract. (And it's interesting to note that a study done by Edward R. Hewitt shows that aquatic insects have a fat content of 15 percent, while minnows weigh in at only 3 percent. This information is as interesting as an example of the richness of human activity as it is useful: imagine that someone would not only think to measure the fat content of a mayfly, but actually go out and do it! The study also indicates why eating a mayfly is worth the trout's effort.)

Remember that trout are carnivores. People who investigate the contents of trout stomachs occasionally turn up some vegetation, but most think this is just the accidental detritus that comes along with the normal food. On the other hand, some people think that trout occasionally like a bit of salad to go with their regular diet. Maybe so, but there are no salad-fly patterns, and no algae flies, either, for that matter. And there would be if trout liked greens.

They are annoyed. This is one explanation of why an attractor fly works. The trout sees a strange apparition floating through his space, and he slashes at it the way a dog snaps at a wasp. Both regret doing it, but neither can resist, sometimes.

They are opportunists. A hatch stimulates feeding because trout understand that a hatch is a temporary phenomenon. They gorge themselves while the gorging is good. A grasshopper or ant suddenly adrift is too good a morsel to pass up. A dace swimming through the trout's lie is worth a short chase. A drifting nymph that passes within reach is there for the taking. Like a duck hunter sitting in his blind, the trout will take what comes, when it comes, assuming he feels like it. And trout have no limits on their take.

They want to. I once stood on a bank of a salmon river in Scotland, gaping into space and not paying attention, when a very large salmon jumped out of the water, danced in the air for a while and then belly-flopped back in. Somewhat amazed, I asked the Scot who was with me why salmon do that sort of thing. "Dunno," he said. "For the hell of it, I guess." That's as good an explanation as any of why a trout bites, sometimes.

Water conditions. In his book *The Ways of Trout*, Leonard Wright theorizes that trout feed when two primary factors come together: water temperature and oxygen levels (which, as we know, are related). Wright notes that a trout's ability to process oxygen is at its highest when the water temperatures is 63 degrees: its gills are most efficient then. In effect, when the water temperature rises or drops dramatically to that optimum, the trout get an oxygen rush that has the same effect as a pre-dinner martini—it stimulates the desire to eat. This is an outstanding example of angling theory. There are few, if any, ways either to refute or prove it, at least from a layman's perspective. It sounds sensible, but who's to say? And so it is an ideal sort of postulation. It proves one thing conclusively—no one is sure what stimulates the urge to eat, at least not sure enough to predict it with certainty. Otherwise there would be no room for interesting theories such as Wright's. That's one of the charms of the sport—one reason why it's an art, not a science.

Wright also notes that trout are more efficient eaters in colder water. That means that the cost/benefit ratio between energy exerted to feed and caloric benefit is greater when the water is colder. When the water temperature is above 63 degrees, trout continue to feed, but they may not be able to convert the food into additional body weight. They eat to maintain themselves. But if the water gets too warm they stop eating altogether, and, in fact, start looking for exits.

Light levels. Trout dislike bright light and will hide from it. This suggests that they would prefer to feed in the morning and evening, and that is a reasonable generalization. But they do need some light to be able to see their food, since they feed primarily by sight. They are therefore less likely to feed actively at night, although this too is a generalization of the broadest possible scope. Bill Willers cites a study of small groups of browns in which 80 percent of the group fed only during the day, while the remainder fed at night. Go figure.

While we're on the subject of light levels, it may be worth repeating the old fishing guide's article of faith that cloudy days are best for the big browns. Here again, the low light levels bring the monsters out from their lairs. At least, that's the hope.

Daily rhythms. This factor is related to light, in the sense that many trout follow a daily pattern of feeding in the morning and in the evening while taking a siesta during the day. Here again, though, the variations are so great that this generalization is barely worth mentioning. In the River Test, for example, the fish become active around nine in the morning and quit at tea time— four in the afternoon. In addition to being very civilized, this behavior largely contradicts the conventional wisdom. On the other hand, this has been my personal experience over a number of years and may be applicable during different times of the year. There are other sections of the same river that may operate differently. It seems that there are as many rhythms in feeding behavior as there are in music.

Individual streams also have rhythms that influence the trout's feeding behavior. At some point in the day, there will be a "drift." The drift is a daily phenomenon which occurs during periods of low light, just before sunrise and just after sunset. Apparently, the drift is nature's way of redistributing stream insects so that population concentrations do not strain the food supplies of a particular section of the stream. At some daily signal, the insects swim or float to just below the surface and then drift with the current until they find a new section of the stream that is less crowded. This is the aquatic equivalent of the flight to the suburbs, and, as in human drift, there is continuing movement as populations concentrate and then move again. This daily drift is most intense as the weather gets warmer and the various insects mature. The drifters consist of the pre-emergence forms of mayflies, caddis, stoneflies, and diptera. Scuds also join in the festivities. The drift can be viewed as a sub-surface hatch: although the insects are not actually hatching, they are moving downstream with the current in sufficient numbers to attract the trout's attention and to stimulate feeding. During a drift, predictable deliveries of food are brought to a predictable spot by the ever reliable current. Small wonder that the trout is territorial. He's like a college student home for vacation, sprawled on the best couch while his mother delivers the milk and cookies.

Even when conditions are favorable, when the light is right and the supply of food is abundant, trout are easily discouraged from feeding—especially by anglers. The term is "putting them down," which describes the result when an angler plops an inelegant cast near a fish and frightens him. Or when the angler splashes and stumbles in the stream or thumps along the bank—or does any of the myriad things that can frighten these timorous creatures. The fish goes down to his holding lie or leaves the area in a flash, and, needless to say, stops eating for a while.

WHERE AND HOW DO TROUT EAT?

The first answer to the first part of this question is, of course, that they eat at their feeding stations. Like a human sitting down at the dinner table, the trout takes up his feeding position and stays there until he's finished—unless he is put down. This feeding station, however, is three-dimensional; it has depth as well as width and length. Depending on the source of the food (winged insects, sub-surface drifters, emerging insects, minnows, and so on), the trout will focus on different depths. And although he may chase a target for a few feet, he will not stray far.

A typical trout stream, if there is such a thing, is not a single entity but rather a group of layered sections. Each section has an approximate beginning, middle, and end. The clearest example of this is a pool. The sections of larger streams may not be so easy to identify. They may be defined by the curves in the river where the action of the water has carved out certain good holding spots or created runs and riffles. No trout stream is uniformly productive from beginning to end or from top to bottom. Rather, it is composed of some sections that offer good trout habitat, strung together with other sections that are not so attractive. (Even a chalk stream such as the Test has certain areas that have better weed growth, more gravel, and better undercut grassy banks than other sections.) And within each section there are numerous three-dimensional feeding stations, each occupied by a trout.

Just as a trout stream has certain sections that are better than others, it also has certain depths at which the trout is more likely to eat. A trout stream, when viewed in cross section, has at least three zones: the bottom, the surface, and the "drift level," or middle area. It has been said that trout feed below the surface at least 90 percent of the time. And of that 90 percent, most of the feeding takes place in the drift level, the area between the bottom and the surface. Not surprisingly, this is the same area that sees the diurnal aquacade known as the daily drift.

Trout also feed along the bottom, and they are not averse to nosing around in the gravel to unearth the nymphs and larvae and pupae that reside there. The point is that, except for a hatch or the occasional terrestrial, most of a trout's food is below the surface, and so it is reasonable that most of a trout's feeding will take place below the surface. Also, the currents differ in force. The current at the bottom is the slowest (because of friction); the current on the surface is fastest. Trout need to conserve energy while feeding, so they generally prefer to stay well below the surface. And, of course, the deeper the trout is, the more secure he feels.

When there is a hatch, the trout will generally move to the surface and take the flies. They may even move to new temporary loca-

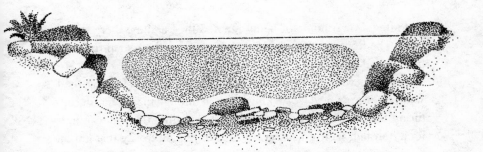

Trout find most of their food in the drift zone, indicated here by the shaded area.

tions close by in order to take greater advantage of a hatch. A trout may move into a pool or a riffle, for example, while a hatch is at its most intense. If he does move, however, he won't generally move very far. After all, he feeds primarily by sight, and needs to see his quarry before beginning the attack. During a hatch, a trout may lose some of his wariness; he can get a little carried away, like a boy at a pie-eating contest. But once the hatch is complete, the trout goes back to his primary feeding and holding station.

As with all other generalizations, however, this one is subject to exceptions. Some streams may be so productive beneath the surface that a hatch raises little if any interest. Trout, in other words, are so busy feeding in the drift zone that they ignore surface insects. Or they may be taking the emergers before they get to the surface and ignoring the insects that do manage to emerge from their shucks and fly off. I've seen this phenomenon on the San Juan River in New Mexico. There was a hatch of mayflies, but very little surface activity. The reason: too much food below the surface, coupled with high and murky water. As a matter of fact, on one such day the trout were feeding at eight and a half feet below the surface. If you could sink a fly to that depth, you could catch them; if you were a few inches higher or lower, you would draw a blank. Either the trout had too much food below the surface or they couldn't see the duns on the surface. Or both. From a trout's point of view, a rich stream is like a river of soup. Many novice anglers throw a dry fly on a stream, and after several hours of being ignored they assume there are no trout. The trout are there, but they're spooning their soup from the bottom and middle of the bowl.

Maybe it would be more accurate to say they're slurping their soup, since trout feed by sucking water in through their mouths, capturing the insect in the flow, and then expelling the water, minus food, through their gills. But it's also important to say that not all takes are the same and not all food ends up in the same part of the trout's eating apparatus. Trout are known, for example, to take bait, such as worms, deep in the throat. In fact, they tend to swallow bait. That's one reason it is difficult for bait fishermen to release their trout unharmed. The trout swallows the worm and the rather large hook, too. Getting the hook out is difficult, if not impossible. A trout will often take an artificial fly, however, in the lip or the jaw or, sometimes, in the tongue. Occasionally, the trout will take a fly deeper than that, perhaps because the act of taking the fly flushed it deeper into the oral cavity than the trout expected. But generally, trout flies are easy to remove. Sometimes the angler may need a hemostat to remove a deeper hook, and sometimes trout will take a fly on the tongue, and the resulting blood smear makes the wound look worse than it probably is (of course, that's easy for me to say, not being the one with a hook in my tongue). But most often, artificial flies are removable with just Adam's pliers. And in all cases, using barbless hooks makes this process easier on all concerned.

The tendency to take flies in the lip or jaw may suggest that trout are more tentative in eating flies than in taking other forms of food, such as worms. This may have some truth to it, but since fly fishermen do not, by definition, use bait, the information is of marginal value. Of greater value, perhaps, is the fact that trout take flies in different ways, depending on species, type of fly, and the trout's mood and degree of hunger at the time. Cutthroat trout, for example, are known to be tentative when they take the fly, whereas brookies, brown trout, and rainbows come at the fly aggressively. Sometimes, especially during a hatch, trout of all species hang just below the surface and rise very gently to sip in the fly. Unlike a boy taking a bath, they hardly leave a ring. Other times they will slash furiously at a fly, even to the point of missing it. Sometimes a hatch will stimulate a feeding frenzy, and the trout will hit the flies with more power than discernment. And sometimes the equally frenzied angler will see a trout rising for a fly, and, with exquisite timing, strike a split second before the trout has the fly, thereby saving himself the trouble of playing the fish.

An angler's eagerness is understandable, because it does seem as if there is only a microsecond available before the trout detects the fact that the fly is a fraud and spits it out. As a general rule, trout do not hook themselves. The angler has to do that by lifting the rod tip at the moment the trout seizes the fly. This action is called the strike, and in many cases it is an all too accurate description of what happens, for the angler as often as not misses the fish as surely as the mighty Casey whiffed in the clutch. (We will go into questions of technique later on, but it's worth mentioning here that the strike does not need to be a violent jerk of the rod. Simply lifting the rod tip will do the trick. After all, the object is to move the fly that fraction of an inch necessary to imbed it in the fish's jaw. The object is not to launch the fish airborne over the angler's head and into the bushes behind.) Even the best anglers only hook up a fraction of the time. Doug Gibson, a man of vast experience on the Henrys Fork and other western rivers, says that you can consider yourself an expert if you hook up 50 percent of the time. Doug also says, if he likes you and he sees you missing a fish, "Don't worry, a worthy fish would have had it." What he means is, "Don't worry. You missed him, but there are more down the way."

Although trout don't always take the same way, they are generally fairly cautious in the way they take, unless overstimulated by a hatch or by a spasm of opportunism such as when an unexpected grasshopper floats by. But while they are cautious, they are also quick—an odd combination that the trout has managed to master. That means the angler not only has to get the fly to float in a natural way, but also has to watch the fly to make sure the fish has actually taken it and still has it before striking. This takes a little practice, and the rule here is that you have to catch fish in order to catch fish. In other words, only the experience—both good and bad—of timing the strike will improve the percentage of hook-ups.

A trout has to see a fly before he can eat it, and that means the fly has to float into his window of vision (if it's a dry fly) or into his subsurface station. It also means the fly has to behave naturally; a fly that acts as though it is not subject to the laws of current will most likely be ignored. And it means the fly design has to be sufficiently accurate or intriguing to outweigh the trout's normal caution and to motivate him to expend some energy. Therefore, the more accurately the angler can present the fly to the trout, the more likely it is that the trout will take it.

Once the trout has seen the fly, however, other factors come into play. First is scent. Trout do make food selections on the basis of scent, but since the only thing most fly fishermen put on their flies is floatant, this information is only one more example of the way the fly fisherman handicaps himself in the name of sport. Admittedly, there are some fly fishermen who add a fishy smell of some sort to their flies, particularly streamers, but most resist the impulse as being unworthy or, as the English say, "not the done thing." Artificial trout flies generally arrive on the water without the added allurement of scent.

A trout also notices the taste and texture of the fly. Fly tiers can't do anything about the taste of their materials—we must assume that everything tastes pretty bad compared to what the trout is expecting when he sips in a fly. All of that underscores the fact that the angler does not have much time to set the hook, because a trout can detect a fraud very quickly, and just as quickly spit it out.

These factors—the trout's essential wariness and quickness combined with the fact that he will use all of his senses to evaluate the fly—mean that dry-fly fishing requires concentration and quick but restrained reactions. In nymph or wet-fly fishing it often means that the angler's sense of feel is critical, because a trout feeding under the surface is often invisible, and sometimes the only way the angler knows he has a take is when he feels the slight tug or some very subtle change in the action of the line. Maybe it's just the fly bouncing on the bottom. Maybe it's the fly snagging in a sunken branch. Or maybe it's a fish. When anglers are fishing nymphs on a chalk stream, they are, if they are following the rules, casting upstream to a known fish; but, even though the water is generally very clear, it is virtually impossible to see a sunken fly as it drifts down to the target fish. The technique then is to strike when you see the white flash of the inside of the trout's mouth. Maybe he is eating your fly, in which case you have a hook-up, or maybe he is chasing something else. You can't expect trout to hook themselves—you have to do that for them, and you don't have any spare time for contemplation. The first time I fished nymphs on the Test, I had the advantage of working with a guide, or as they say there, a gillie. When the moment came to strike, more often than not I was staring dull-wittedly into the water searching for the fly, and it fell to Jim, the gillie, to advise me. He would say, in effect, "You may strike now, sir," and I would, and there would be a fish—much to my surprise, because I couldn't see the fly or the take. The fact that it was raining and water was pouring off my glasses added a degree of difficulty, but that was counterbalanced by Jim's long years of experience in watching for the white flash. (Jim's exact words, now that I think about it, were somewhat less genteel: "He's chewing it, for God's sake. Strike, man, strike!")

Anglers encounter similar problems when they use tiny dry flies—size 20 and smaller. When a small fly bounces through the riffles, with the sun reflecting off the water and the fly dipping and dodging in the current, even Superman would have trouble seeing it. In those cases, the angler strikes when he sees a rise near where he thinks the fly should be. Sometimes he is rewarded.

THE GREAT CATCH-AND-RELEASE DEBATE

I mentioned earlier that trout sometimes seem to take flies without much enthusiasm. They come up and look and perhaps very tentatively have a nibble. That could be because they are not hungry. Or it could be because they've seen these fraudulent offerings before, and they remember. Trout may not be very intelligent, but they are not complete dimwits. They do learn. And when they're caught, lifted into a boat or up on shore, they do recall the experience. No doubt the memory fades after a while, but no one is sure exactly how long it takes.

The fact that trout remember the experience of being caught is the primary fuel in the catch-and-release debate. Of course, among American fly fishermen, there really isn't much of a debate. The prevailing ethic is catch and release. No fly fisherman seriously disputes the idea that not killing the trout we catch is good for the sport. In fact, the practice has been so successful in providing (and in some cases restoring) good trout fishing around the country that it has acquired the force of morality. Certainly it is one crucial distinction between fly fishermen and most bait fishermen. Indeed, there is even a certain priggishness about some of the strongest advocates of catch and release. I remember fishing for bonefish in the Bahamas, and my guide was a slender local boy of about eighteen. He and his family liked to eat bonefish. That in itself was a surprise to me, because I had always heard they were more culinary trouble than they were worth, but he liked them. We caught a couple of nice six-pounders and he asked me if he could keep them. Of course, I agreed. When we went back to the fishing lodge for dinner, one of the other guests looked in our boat and when he saw the fish he got very huffy indeed. That, it seemed to me at the time, was carrying the catch-and-release issue to a new level. And the fact that we then went in to a very fine dinner of grilled tuna did nothing to lessen this fellow's sense of moral outrage. Irony is often lost on zealots.

Despite the obvious benefits of catch and release, not everyone agrees that it's such a uniformly good thing. In addition to a skinny Bahamian with a taste for bonefish, there are legions of British anglers who think catch and release is destructive. If it were not for the fact that this debate sheds light on the trout's behavior, it would only be another example of Shaw's dictum that Americans and British are two peoples separated by a common language. But the debate *is* relevant because it highlights a couple of key points.

First, trout do remember, and they are therefore harder to catch the more often they are caught and the longer they survive. Second, they are territorial. It is no wonder, then, that the British dislike catch and release, for they labor under a shortage of resources; there just aren't that many productive trout streams. In fact, most of the good water is owned or leased and the fishing is therefore private. If you owned, say, a quarter of a mile of the Test, and that was the only spot on the river you could fish, you would be concerned about the growing sophistication of your resident trout. After all, because trout are territorial, they are likely to stay in all the good holding lies until someone comes along and evicts them. And since they remember being caught, they will gradually become harder and harder to catch, and they will reach the point, at least theoretically, when it's impossible to catch them. At that point, your property that once was a trout stream is now just scenery.

The British have a solution for this problem: keep a few now and then and thereby open up the holding spots for immigrants from other parts of the river. And, perhaps, add a few stockers to supplement the population.

The phenomenon of overeducated trout has occurred in certain American streams, such as the Letort in central Pennsylvania. The Letort is a limestone stream (much like the British chalk streams in composition), and has a section reserved exclusively for catch-and-release fly fishing. This stretch is only about a mile or so long. The fish in that section know the names of the trout flies better than the anglers who are throwing them. It is tough fishing.

Trout that have been caught several times understandably get a little shy and cut back on their feeding. That can lead to undersized, scrawny, and unhealthy fish. Then, too, the effort of fighting, often vainly, against the hook and the pull of the rod and line, can tire fish to the point that it takes quite a while to recover. In fact, occasionally a fish will wear himself out completely and, when he comes to the net, will not revive. He simply rolls over and calls it quits.

The implications of all of this information are several. First, catch and release is without question a good idea. It protects the resources for everyone and allows us to stay on the stream all day regardless of how many fish we catch. But catch and release works best in areas where there is plenty of water and not so many anglers. Obviously, in big rivers with lots of fish, the odds of catching the same one too often are very small, and the general trout population remains ignorant of the risks of taking a fly. Even fish that are caught will forget as time goes by. But in smaller rivers where there are fewer resident fish, such as the Letort and Test, keeping a fish now and then could have a beneficial effect on the total population, since new fish would move into the spot vacated by the martyrs. Still, as a general policy, catch and release is unassailable as a key foundation to good management of trout water. It is not, however, the basis of a new religion. We fly fishermen would do well, I think, to avoid a holier-than-thou attitude when discussing fishing with our brothers of the worm and spoon and with our cousins from across the sea.

What about the fact that sometimes a trout will not survive after being hooked? It's a shame, but it happens. All you can do is minimize these accidents by not overplaying the fish and by returning it to the water as fast as possible in the manner suggested below. If the fish dies, take it home and eat it. And enjoy it. Killing and eating a fish is not the final act of *Hamlet*.

When you do release the fish, try to minimize the damage as you remove the hook. If the hook is too deeply imbedded, you may have to cut the leader and leave the hook where it is. A trout can generally live (though, one assumes, not happily) with a hook in its mouth. Over time the hook rusts away, and trout are pretty tough. I once caught a good-sized rainbow on the San Juan that had two flies and a leader dangling from its anal cavity. The fish was feisty and healthy, even after having passed that collection through its system. One thing is sure—if you don't put the fish back, it will not live.

Reviving a fish basically entails letting him get some oxygen into his system, and the technique is generally to hold him by the tail and pull him gently back and forth to let the water work through his gills. Or you can hold him with his nose into the current until he's ready to go back to work. When he is, he will leave.

The catch-and-release discussion is one facet of a larger continuing debate about the best ways to manage natural resources. A useful lesson to take away from the whole thing is that the most obvious solutions and explanations are not necessarily the best, nor are they always correct for all situations. If the Brits do not take some fish out of their limited stretches of river, they will eventually have no fishing. Unyielding catch-and-release policies are ultimately destructive in that environment. This whole issue is reminiscent of discussions about stocking trout water. In his lovely book *Where the Bright Waters Meet*, Harry Plunket-Greene talks about his club's destruction—through stocking—of the Bourne, which is a small tributary of the Test. They wanted to improve the fishing, so they stocked the stream. But there simply wasn't enough food or habitat for the numbers of trout they introduced, and the entire stream was degraded. The fish starved. That was around the turn of the century. We know a little more now about habitat management, but we don't know everything.

CHAPTER 6

Equipment Basics

Thou shalt say unto Aaron, Take thy rod and cast it...
—Exodus

*So my brother and I learned to cast Presbyterian-style,
on a metronome.*
—Norman Maclean, *A River Runs Through It*

ARON'S ROD WAS NOT A FLY ROD. Nor was it a spinning
rod, for that matter. But he was ordered to cast it, and in
so doing he did end up with a few scaly creatures. And so he could
be nominated as the first patron saint of fishing, though it's a
stretch, since Aaron's scaly creatures were serpents. How an Old
Testament Hebrew would feel about being a patron saint is another question. And, as long as we're on the subject of the Old
Testament, we should not forget the story of Jonah, whom David
James Duncan in his book *The River Why* called the "human fly."
All of this is just more proof that fly fishing is a venerable and ecu-
menical sport.

Be that as it may, the rod is obviously a key element in fly fishing. But the important thing to remember is that it's only a tool. Fly
fishing is not just fly *casting*. Casting is a means to the end, not the
end in itself. While that may seem stunningly obvious, my observations over the years have led me to conclude that not everyone
actually believes it.

I will confess that the line quoted above from *A River Runs
Through It* has never made sense to me, and I was raised a

Presbyterian. The puzzling thing is that Norman Maclean knew perfectly well that a fly rod and line were just delivery mechanisms. While a metronome goes back and forth, back and forth tirelessly, a fly rod should not, any more than a mailman should make a dozen trips up and down your walkway before delivering the bills and catalogues. The object of the cast is to get the fly near the trout without frightening him and putting him off his feed. The idea, in other words, is to get the fly on the water, not to see how long we can wave the rod and line artfully in the air. Even the acrobatic rainbow trout will not leap fifteen feet above the water to grab a fly that's whipping back and forth with lunatic gaiety.

This whipping of the line through the air is called false casting, and it has a purpose in certain cases, as we will discuss. But here's the key—false casting is not synonymous with fly casting. Any fly fishing guide in the world will tell you that the less false casting you do, the better. Why? Because the more time the fly spends in the air, the less time it spends in the water, which is where the fish reside. Also, as long as the line is flying back and forth, a plaything of the wind, it has the chance to tie itself in knots or wrap itself around your ears and subject you to the embarrassment that always attends self-inflicted muddles, to say nothing of self-inflicted hook wounds. The back-and-forth action of a metronome is not a good image to keep in your mind as you practice the art of presenting a fly to a fish.

Maybe Maclean was trying to suggest that good fly casters have a grooved stroke, the same way a hitter in baseball or a golfer has a stroke that he repeats every time with slight adjustments for conditions. That's certainly true, but here again the image of the metronome is troubling, because metronomes have an arm that waves back and forth at equal angles to the perpendicular. Those angles seem to be at about ten o'clock and two o'clock. That's not such a good stroke—at least not for today's rod materials.

Fly casting is based on one essential truth which clarifies all the mechanical theory about casting technique and even rod design:

We are casting the line, not the fly. The fly is attached to the end of the line, but is only a passenger, and like a leaf in the current, it will go where it's taken.

An average trout fly is virtually weightless. If you open your fly box in a stiff breeze, some of the flies will blow away, and as you grab for them—and then immediately wish you hadn't—you're reminded of how little mass these things contain. (We'll put aside the problem of weighted flies for the time being.) The implication is that you cannot use the weight of the fly itself when trying to propel it toward the quarry.

If you pick up an average fly line, you'll notice that it does have some mass. It has the approximate diameter of vermicelli. It's made of a relatively heavy synthetic material. If you wanted to make a lariat loop and jump through it, you could, or if you wanted to string it between two trees and hang out the wash, you could do that, too.

Fly casting, therefore, is the opposite of bait or spin casting. In those heresies, the bait or spoon or jig or whatever has weight, and the line is a barely visible, virtually weightless nylon monofilament. To cast such a rig, the angler uses the weight of the lure to bend the rod, and then slings the lure out onto the water. In fly casting, since the lure has no weight, we need something that will bend the rod sufficiently to generate enough power to sling the fly forward. That's the function of the line—to bend the rod back and thereby load it with the power necessary to shoot the whole rig forward at the right time and in the right direction. Just to dramatize the difference, consider this—you can practice fly casting without a fly attached to your line. Most people do practice that way, in fact. But you could never practice spin casting or bait casting without a lure tied to the monofilament line. You might as well try to throw a cobweb. The key to all casting, then, is to get the rod to flex. In bait or spin casting, the weight of the lure does the job; in fly casting, it's the weight of the line.

People who have been around for more than three decades may remember the stiff poles that athletes used to wield in the pole vault. They were thick aluminum, and as the vaulter dashed down the runway and inserted the pole into the box, he felt a shock to his system, because that pole had about as much give as a skinflint uncle. As a result, if the pole vaulter had not generated enough energy through the speed of his run-up, there was no vault. Only a jarring collision. The key to the event was strength—the ability to pull one's body up as that pole ever so slowly arced rigidly up and balanced on its end while the vaulter arched over the bar and then fell, hoping that the pole had already dropped to the side. But then somebody developed the fiberglass pole, and the sport (and records) changed overnight. The new poles were slender, flexible wands, and the keys to the business became timing and speed rather than brute strength. The vaulter still ran down the runway at top speed, but at the moment of impact, he simply held on while the pole bent back nearly double and then at last shot straight again, propelling the vaulter over the bar and, with luck, onto a Wheaties box.

If you want a mental image of the mechanics of fly casting, think of the modern day pole vaulter rather than the metronome. The rod is the pole. The power to propel is in the initial backward flex and the subsequent forward thrust of the rod. And the weight that creates the flex is the fly line. The key is timing, just as in the pole vault. Once airborne, the vaulter waits, waits, waits until the pole is fully loaded with energy, fully flexed. Then he starts his own forward motion, or lift, and coordinates it with the forward thrust of the pole as it unflexes.

Similarly, the fly caster uses the line to "load" the rod. The fly caster lifts the line off the water and throws it back over his shoulder, stopping the rod just about when it's vertical, and he waits, waits, waits until the line pays out behind him and the weight of the line pulls back on the rod and flexes it, bends it backwards to its most efficient degree of flex. Then, when the line is virtually straight behind him and the rod is flexed to its optimum, the caster brings the rod forward. The coordinated motion shoots the line toward the target. It is not strength so much as timing; the power resides in the flex of the rod, not "in the muscles of your brawny arms." (In fact, this reference to Longfellow underscores the main point, for if someone says you cast like a blacksmith, you should not take it as a compliment, probably.)

Here, then, is the key to fly casting:

Let it load.

As a line, this may not be on a par with "Call me Ishmael," but it is one of the rare generalizations in fly fishing that is always true. Let it be your mantra.

We'll go into some more detail on casting later on, but we first need to spend a little time on the tools of the trade. Aside from the fly, there are four elements in the fly fisherman's basic arsenal: rod, reel, line and leader. Of this quartet, the least understood is probably the leader, so it might be wise to start there.

The Leader

It is generally a bad thing for a country when its leader is weak, and it is a similarly bad thing for an angler when his leader is weak, for a good fish will break a weak leader just as surely as a vote of no confidence will send an ineffectual prime minister into retirement. That said, however, it must also be said that in fly fishing the leader is by definition the weakest link in the chain that connects the angler to the fish. If anything goes wrong during an encounter with a good fish, it will most likely happen somewhere in the leader. All leaders are weak; some are just weaker than others.

The leader is a piece of monofilament—thin, clear, nylon line— that attaches to the fly line and forms the connection to the fly. The fly, in other words, is tied to the leader, not to the fly line. The leader may be anywhere from six feet to fifteen feet long, and it tapers from its thickest section (called the butt), which is tied to the fly line, to the thinnest section, which is called the tippet. Generally, you will start with a leader at the beginning of the day, and if things go according to plan, you will still be using *most* of the same piece of monofilament at the end of the day. You will, however, probably have changed the tippet—the last eighteen inches or so of the leader—several times, either because some fish broke it (the tippet is the thinnest, weakest part of the leader) or because you inadvertently threw a fly into the trees or bushes and were forced to break the tippet yourself. And there are other reasons to change the tippet, as we shall see.

The purpose of the leader is to separate the fly from the fly line, which as we know is thick and therefore rather obvious to a fish. The leader allows us to present a fly to a fish without showing him the fly line. Its primary purpose is to aid in the deception.

What else is there to know about leaders? Well, for one thing, they come in several categories, and typically, the numbering system does not at first make much sense. For example, the thickest, and therefore strongest, leader is labeled 0X, the next thickest 1X, and so on until we arrive at the most anemic of all, the 8X, a leader so delicate that it seems to belong to the realm of vapors rather than solids. It always seemed to me that this numbering system was backwards, and that the higher the number the stronger the leader should be. But, no. It is the other way around. Only one person has ever been able to explain this to me, and I offer his idea as a useful way of keeping this stuff straight. He said, in essence, this: in the old days of fishing in England, the leaders were made of gut. And since the diameter of the gut was relatively uniform and fairly thick, a new leader would need to be tapered in order to be useful in fooling trout. The angler would taper the gut by drawing it through a kind of jeweler's tool, and each time he drew it through more of the exterior would be shaved off. Thus, drawing it through one time (1X) shaved very little, whereas drawing it through, say, six times (6X) left him with a considerably thinner and more delicate leader. And so on. Hence the numbering system.

I would like to give credit to the man who explained this to me, but I have forgotten who it was. Whether his explanation is correct or not, I cannot say, but I have always found it a useful way to remember which leaders are which. More and more, modern manufacturers are also printing a leader's breaking strength, in pounds, on the package. But they all still use the "X" terminology, too, and most guides and serious anglers still think in terms of X's rather than breaking strength. It is part of the esoterica of the sport.

Further, there are stronger leaders (stronger than 0X) which are used for fish other than trout, and these are labeled by their breaking strength, or pound test.

The X system also tells you the diameter of the material, if you remember The Rule of 11. Subtract the X designation from 11, and you get the material's thickness in thousandths of an inch. A 4X tippet, for instance, has a diameter of .007 inch; 11 minus 4 equals 7.

Since a leader tapers from the butt section down to the tippet, it follows that every leader will have different strength at different points; i.e., the butt section will be the strongest, and the tippet will be the weakest. Some manufacturers make leaders in a single strand that tapers evenly from the butt to the end of the tippet. Other manufacturers provide leaders made from sections knotted together. Some anglers like to construct their own leaders by knotting together several strands of monofilament of different diameters.

When you buy a new leader, the package will quite logically state the breaking strength of the weakest part, i.e., the tippet. Throughout the day, as you tie on new flies or break off pieces of tippet, you will need to add some new material. You will probably try to match the original construction of the leader, though there is no need to be too precise about this. If the original tippet was a 5X, you can replace it with 4X or a 6X without noticeable difficulties. The object is to create the effect of a tapered monofilament, not because it is aesthetically better, but because a tapered distribution of mass allows the leader to "turn over" smoothly when it is cast. We will get into casting technique later on, but it might be worthwhile to explain this turning over phenomenon.

When you cast a fly line, the forward motion of the rod shoots the line toward the target. As it flies forward, the leading edge of the line forms what is called the loop. Seen from the side, this loop looks like a paper clip with only one closed end, that part being the loop. The open end is the end of the line with the leader and the fly. This loop continues forward until all the fly line is straight in front of the caster and all that remains of the loop is the leader. If the leader is not properly constructed and balanced it could collapse at this point, or in the terminology of the sport, not turn over. The result will be a pile of leader plopping inelegantly down. Any fish interested in eating the fly would have to untangle it first from the bird's nest of monofilament surrounding it, and there aren't many fish willing to go to the trouble.

Your choice of leader will be determined primarily by the water in which you are fishing. Since the leader is the weakest link in the chain of tackle, most anglers prefer to use a relatively short, strong leader, but that is sometimes not possible. In spring creeks and chalk streams, for example, where the water is clear and the surface is flat and unmarred by obvious currents, an angler needs a long and delicate leader, especially if he is fishing dry flies. Short, thicker leaders are simply too visible to wary trout who have a good view of the entire proceedings. From the trout's perspective, the underside of smooth water looks like a mirror, and when a short, thick leader lands on this mirror, it creates a noticeable splash and flash that can put skittish trout off their feed in an instant. A long, delicate leader is the price of admission to chalk-stream success. This type of fishing is called "far and fine," because the casts tend to be somewhat longer and the line and leader much more delicate than those used on more broken water. On runoff streams, the action of the water hides the leader to some extent, and the angler can get by with a shorter and stronger leader. Similarly, when the water is clouded, an angler can use a shorter, less delicate leader.

Leader selection also depends to some extent on the type of flies you are using. A fifteen-foot 8X leader will simply not be able to handle a large, heavy, wind-resistant fly. It will not be able to turn over. Fortunately, most spring-creek fishing is done with smaller flies, and especially with dry flies, although nymphs have their adherents. And, speaking of wind, it will come as no surprise to learn that long, wispy leaders do not do well in the wind.

When it comes to leaders, length and strength are functions of the water you are fishing and the conditions you encounter. The more educated the trout and the better their ability to see, the farther and finer you must fish.

Speaking of leader strength, it's worth noting that leaders have relatively short life spans, not unlike mayflies. This is especially true of tippet material. This stuff is inexpensive and should be replaced at least yearly, though many anglers are reluctant to throw anything away, especially something that hasn't been used. I have some spools of tippet material that have been around for more than a decade—veritable tippet Methuselahs. I should throw all of it away, and I will someday. But in the meantime I know enough not to use it.

A Brief Digression on the 100-Percent Knot

In the Middle Ages scientists dreamed of the Philosopher's Stone, the one missing ingredient that would allow them to convert base metal into gold. Today's scientists dream of the Single Theory, the formula that will explain everything, at least everything having to do with physics. Whether our scientists' quest is any less chimerical than their medieval counterparts' remains to be seen. But quests—and the people who embark upon them—are interesting in and of themselves. Not surprisingly, fly fishing has its own set of careworn but undiscouraged seekers. These are the anglers searching for the 100-percent knot, which is a knot as strong as the unknotted material in which it is tied. While some claim to have come close, the current thinking is that no one has truly developed—or, perhaps, discovered would be the better word—the 100-percent knot.

What is the meaning of this bit of information? That some people have strange interests? Yes, but we knew that already. That tying knots in material weakens the overall strength of the material? Yes, that's the real point. If there's no such thing as a 100-percent knot, it follows that any knot necessarily weakens the material. What's more, the only place where we intentionally tie knots is in the leader—which by definition is the weakest link in the chain of equipment. The implication, therefore, is that we should try to minimize the number of knots that we put in the leader. That implies, in turn, that the leader should contain only those knots that we actually want to be there, such as the knot that joins the tippet to the rest of the leader or the knots that join the various sections of the leader. Well, of course, you say—how would knots appear in a leader unless we tied them ourselves? The sad truth is that knots often do appear in leaders as though by magic. One moment we are casting a pristinely knotless leader. The next moment we examine it there is a tiny knot (worse yet, several) glistening along its length. These are called wind knots, and if your leader (most probably your tippet) has even one such knot in it, that will be its weakest point. When a good fish bites the fly and runs or jumps or shakes his head in furious displeasure at the hook, chances are the leader will break, and what's more, chances are that the break will come at the wind knot—because the wind has not discovered the 100-percent knot, and what's more, is indifferent to the quest.

What is to be done? Well, the best idea is to avoid wind knots in the first place. As advice this ranks alongside "buy low, sell high"—undeniably true but not very helpful. The question is *how*. One way is to minimize false casting, for it is while the line and leader are in the air that wind knots materialize. This seems simple enough, but there is something about false casting that exerts a siren call on some anglers, especially people new to the game. I once watched a novice angler on the Madison River in Montana. He was well decked out and could have passed for veteran, but on the water he gave away his fledgling status by routinely, hypnotically throwing eight false casts before letting the line drop to the water. And as soon as the fly hit the water, it immediately began to drag (i.e., the line was swept away by the current and dragged the fly sideways), whereupon he picked it up and resumed false casting. The fish, of course, ignored his fly. After a while he sat down, and you could almost see him beginning to wonder why people make a fuss over fly fishing, for it really wasn't much fun. And no doubt after all that false casting his leader was a garland of gleaming wind knots, each vying with its fellows to be the first to break in the event, albeit unlikely, that a fish was able to seize the fly before it resumed its flight. Moral of the story: minimize false casting. You will spend more time fishing and less time untangling or replacing leaders and tippets.

In reality, "wind knot" is a misnomer. The knots are primarily caused by faulty casting technique. (More on casting later.) But the point about false casting remains valid: the fewer false casts you make, the less chance you have to make a mess of your leader.

One last thought on leaders and wind knots—check your tippet every now and then. When you find a wind knot, change the tippet. You won't want to, because it's a bother. But if you don't, you're likely to be sorry when a good fish takes your fly, because he'll probably keep it.

An Even Briefer Digression on Knots In General

*A train left New York traveling at sixty MPH carrying
three tons of coal, four nuns and a traveling salesman...*
—*Algebra for Fun and Profit*

It is, in my opinion, impossible to learn how to tie knots from reading a book. Even illustrations of the knots provide no help—at least in my experience. These instructions and illustrations are the close cousins of those awful word problems we used to toil over in math class. I vowed I would never do another word problem, and I am proud to say I have kept that vow. More recently, I also vowed I would never again study a knot diagram, for nothing but frustration and indigestion ever follows such an effort. Therefore, no more will be said on the subject of word problems or knots, except this—all anglers need to know a few basic knots. There is the knot that attaches the tippet to the hook, the knot that connects various sections of leader (e.g., the tippet to the rest of the leader) and the knot that attaches the butt of the leader to the fly line. The best way to learn these knots is to get someone to show you how to tie them.

The Line

*Come live with me, and be my love, And we will some
    new pleasure prove
Of golden sands, and crystal brooks, With silken lines,
    and silver hooks.*

> —John Donne, "The Bait"

It seems that even in the seventeenth century anglers used fishing
metaphors when they went a-wooing. And I would like to see
some unattached angler use this line on a lissome female at a
roadhouse hard by a trout river, sort of as an attractor. I think it
could work. (Later in this same poem, Donne says: "...curious
traitors, sleavesilke flies Bewitch poore fishes wandering eyes,"
which suggests that the poet knew trout were sight feeders. It is
not surprising, therefore, that Donne's biographer was Izaak
Walton, himself.) But, be that as it may, the real reason I include
this quote is because it mentions silken lines. Yes, the lines did
used to be made of silk, and what a lot of bother they were.
Modern science has relieved us of some of the many annoyances
that used to be associated with old-fashioned equipment, such as
constantly greasing the fly line so that it would float. Today's
lines are synthetic; they float better than Banquo's Ghost. So science has come to our rescue and provided us with synthetic lines
that are durable and buoyant and easy to maintain. But scientific
advances always carry a cost, for no one would walk up to someone and say "come with me and be my love and we will some new
pleasure prove of golden sands and crystal brooks with plastic-
coated HY-Float lines and barbless hooks." As poetry, the new
lines are a failure. But they are a lot easier to use than the stuff
our ancestors struggled with.

The other major advantage of the new synthetic lines—beyond
the fact that they are hardy and float well when asked—is that they
are super smooth. They run through the guides on the rods with just
a whisper of resistance, and they shoot toward the target effortlessly when properly cast.

Lines are like flies in that they are divided into those that are supposed to float and those that are supposed to sink. There is a third category composed of lines which have multiple personalities—just the tip of the line sinks while the rest floats. Not surprisingly, these are called sinking-tip lines. Some lines sink fast, others sink slowly. Depending on their density, these are called fast-sinking, slow-sinking, or intermediate lines. It is curious that the angling industry, which is so creative when it comes to naming flies, is so unimaginative when it comes to naming lines. It may be because flies are designed and named by individuals, whereas lines are manufactured by companies. There may be a lesson there somewhere.

Floating lines are, of course, used for dry-fly fishing, but they can also be used to fish wet flies and nymphs, because while the line floats, the leader can sink, especially if the fly is weighted in some fashion. Flies can be weighted either by constructing them with some metal parts (a strand of wire wrapped around the hook, or a metal bead at the head of the fly) or by adding a piece of split shot (a spherical piece of lead) to the leader. This split shot is generally attached about six to twelve inches above the fly, and it makes casting more difficult and much less enjoyable. The extra weight exerts downward force on the line; if your timing is off, the chances of the line collapsing behind you are greatly improved, if that is the right word. And the chances of hooking yourself or your near neighbors is also enhanced. For this reason, casting weighted flies is often called "chuck and duck." No one likes doing it, but sometimes it is necessary because the fish are feeding well below the surface, and they are regally indifferent to your preference for dry-fly fishing. When chucking and ducking, it is well to wear a sturdy hat.

But the point is that you can fish relatively deep waters using a floating line. For example, in the San Juan River in winter, when the water is high and murky and there is nary a rise in sight, people fish floating lines with long leaders by attaching weight to the leader and determining exactly how deep the fish are (by trial and error and angler cooperation). They then use a leader that is exactly that length (or depth) and attach a "strike indicator" to the end of the line, i.e., at the point where the leader meets the fly line. This strike indicator is just a mass of yarn that is treated with a substance that helps it to float. The strike indicator in turn helps the fly line to float and supports the sunken leader, so that the leader and weighted fly settle into an up-and-down attitude, and the fly swims with the current at the desired depth. The angler then fixes his eyes on the strike indicator and strikes at the slightest twitch. It may be the fly touching bottom, or it may be a fish sampling the fly. There's no way to tell, so anglers fishing this way strike early and often, like the Teamsters in the Fifties.

There are those who deride this sort of fishing. They say using a strike indicator this way is no different from using a bobber which, after all, serves exactly the same functions—to support the weight of the lure and hold the line perpendicular to the surface and to indicate when there is a strike. People who say this are correct. And there is no doubt what the ancient members of the ancient English dry-fly clubs would have thought of this business. But sometimes there is no alternative, other than staying home.

Even with a floating line, however, it's not always necessary to use weight to fish a wet fly. Nymph patterns are designed not to float, and will sink once they have been thoroughly soaked. When a nymph sinks it pulls the leader with it. The leader is just monofilament—light enough to stay afloat if the fly floats, but too slender to resist being dragged under if the fly sinks. Even an unweighted nymph, once it is thoroughly wet, will pull most of the leader under. The nymph can then bounce quite nicely along the bottom of a shallow riffle or hang in the drift zone of deeper water, even though you are using a floating line. Similarly, emerger patterns that imitate insects struggling free from their nymphal shucks are also tied not to float well, but rather to sink just below the surface film. You fish these patterns with a floating line. Weight, either in the fly or on the line, is necessary only when you want to get down deep and get there quickly.

It is generally agreed that a floating line is the most useful, and it's clearly the favored line of all right-thinking trout anglers. Sinking lines are used when fishing in lakes, or in deep pools below dams or in deep rivers. The quarry then is often oversize lake trout or the giant browns that lurk in the depths and never rise to the surface. The only way to catch them is to go down after them, and in these cases a sinking line may be the only choice, since even a heavily weighted fly will not be able to drag a floating line deep enough. (We're talking *deep*.) But in my opinion a person may fish quite happily throughout an entire angling career and never use a sinking line—and not miss it. Casting a sinking line is for me a joyless experience. It hardly seems like fly fishing, except that you use a fly rod. But there is no "presentation" of the fly involved in the business. It's a matter of getting lots of line in the water, letting it sink, and then stripping it back in by hand, a foot or so at a time, and then repeating the process over and over. It's a sport for someone of a particularly contemplative habit of mind who has a great deal of patience and a boat.

Like leaders, lines are described with a numbering system. And, not surprisingly, the numbering system is just the opposite of the system for leaders. Whereas leaders go from 0X to 8X, with the lowest number being the strongest, lines go from 1 to 12, with the lowest number being the lightest. In other words, the higher the number, the greater the weight of the line.

The heavier the line, the easier it is to throw a heavy, wind-resistant fly or cast into the teeth of a gale—assuming, of course, that the line is matched with a rod designed for it. A 9-weight line will throw a bigger or heavier fly than a 4-weight line because it has more mass, and, therefore, more foot-pounds of energy in flight. Since a person is capable of moving the line only so fast, the only way to cast a heavier or more wind-resistant fly (that is, to do more foot-pounds of work) is to sling a line with greater mass.

Most trout anglers find that they use only a couple of different line weights. A 4-weight line is about the lightest that most people use, and a 7-weight about the heaviest. You simply don't need the heavier lines because trout flies are, by and large, relatively light and streamlined—compared, say, to a deer-hair mouse used for bass fishing or an epoxy crab used for bonefish. These heavier, more air-resistant flies require heavier lines to propel them. But trout flies can be fired with lighter artillery. And the lighter the line, the less disturbance it creates when it lands on the water. For that reason, anglers who fish spring creeks chalk streams tend to use lighter lines (4 and 5 weights) because the presentation of the fly needs to be delicate. On the other hand, any line much lighter than a 4 weight can pose some problems when the wind blows, for such lines are so light that, when you ask them to fly into headwinds, they simply "down tools" and refuse. Further, extremely light lines have some difficulty propelling larger trout flies, especially those that have a bit of weight attached.

On bigger rivers and broken water, the action of the current creates a constant disturbance on the surface, which conceals the impact of the line to some degree. Anglers can then use heavier lines, such as 6 and 7 weights. Sometimes they have little choice in the matter, since on big rivers the wind has more room to operate, and it takes advantage of the opportunity. An angler therefore needs to use a heavier line just so he can cast beyond his own shadow.

So, you need to match the line weight with the type of stream, weather conditions, and type of fly you are using. Conditions may not always allow you to use the perfect combination. It does get windy on a spring creek now and then, and even though you would like to cast a size 18 dry fly with a light line and long leader, the weather may force you to compromise. In other words, the same logic operates in the selection of fly lines as in the selection of leaders.

Sensibly, rods and lines have the same numbering system. A rod is designed and manufactured to be used with a specific line weight, and is therefore described in the same terms—a 4-weight rod is designed for a 4-weight line. If you were to put a 9-weight line on the rod, you could perhaps cast it, but much less efficiently than with a 9-weight rod, that is, a rod designed to throw a 9-weight line. As a rule, the heavier the line, the heavier and sturdier the rod.

This is just common sense, since a heavier line requires greater strength in the rod. A heavy line will, of course, flex a light rod, but the rod will not respond efficiently: the line will overpower the rod and the cast will collapse. It would be like trying to shoot a rocket with a bow; a bow works fine with an arrow, but for a heavier missile you need a heavier launcher. Rod manufacturers—the good ones, at least—spend a lot of time and money trying out new materials and designs in order to improve the coordination between rod and line. Of course, all of their careful calculations are thrown out the window when you add weight to the fly—the balance between rod and line is upset. But that is why such casting is called "chuck and duck"—the basic mechanics of the rod and line are disrupted. (Even so, most modern rods are strong enough to adjust—as long as the caster's technique is sufficient to the task.)

Someone new to the game of fly fishing for trout—someone trying to decide which rod to buy—is usually advised to get a 6-weight outfit. That is probably the most versatile of all rigs. It is light enough for most conditions, but heavy enough to cast larger flies in difficult weather. On the other hand, new anglers should be forewarned that they will buy more than one rod. It is inevitable. Rods proliferate like barn cats. One day you will have just one; a few short years later, you will have a profusion. So the choice of the first one is not critical. And every time you buy a new rod, you will also buy a new reel designed especially to carry the appropriate line, and, of course, you will also buy the line that goes with the rod.

Given the certainty that you will continually spend money on rods, reels and lines, you may be in the mood to seek economies wherever possible. If so, you might give some thought to the type of line you buy—beyond the issues of line weight and floatability. These days you really only have to worry about two different types of lines. The first is called weight forward. This line (regardless of its weight) is constructed so that the first 30 or so feet of the line are thicker and heavier than the remainder of the line. If you spread the entire line on the ground, one end would be noticeably thicker than the other—rather like a marsh cattail, though not that pro-

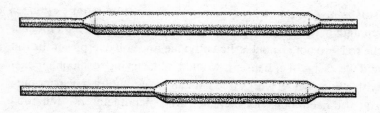

Some anglers prefer a double-taper line (top) because it's easier to control on the water than a weight-forward line is, and because it can be reversed when one end becomes worn. But the weight-forward design (bottom) is more popular nowadays, mostly because it makes distance casting easier.

nounced. Many people believe that these weight-forward lines make casting a little easier, since the heavier section pulls the thinner section as an engine pulls a caboose.

The other type of line is called the double taper. In this design, both ends of the line are slimmer than the middle, and the middle is far longer than either end. Moreover, the two ends are exactly the same. That means that the angler can fish with this line using one end until it frays (for lines, like the anglers who use them, eventually wear out) and then turn the line around and use the other end. Therein lies the potential for economy. This is, of course, little more than self delusion for many people, because the least expensive item in the troika of rod, reel, and line is the line. And it seems a little inconsistent to worry about extending the life of a forty-dollar line when you are spending hundreds on rods and reels.

Still, it is undeniable that a double-taper line has the potential to give roughly twice the length of service as a weight-forward line. This is the kind of information that many anglers find useful when discussing expenditures with their partners in life's travails: "Yes, it is true that I just spent two thousand on a split-cane four-weight rod, but I think of that as an investment. What you probably don't realize is that I bought a double-taper line to go with it." It is the sort of argument that stops the opposition cold, because it not only implies financial sagacity but also uses jargon that is unintelligible to the non-angler in the sketch. (This technique does not work when both partners are anglers, but when both are anglers, challenges about equipment expenses do not arise, since both understand that rod and reel collections must inevitably grow.)

The other advantage I have noticed with the double-taper line is that it is easier in some ways to handle. When I want to adjust the way the line is lying on the water or adjust it to prevent the current from dragging the fly (this adjustment is called mending, on which more later), the heavier middle section of a double-taper line makes the maneuver easier than does the thin middle section of a weight-forward line.

Still, despite its many virtues, most people reject the double-taper line for the weight-forward. For the (mythical) trout fisherman who only wants one rod, reel, and line, a 6-weight rod with a floating, weight-forward line would probably be the choice.

Lines come in a variety of colors. Floating lines especially have a wide range of choices, most of them tending toward the garish—or the stylish, depending on how you feel about neon. The garish colors are supposed to be easier to see, I assume, and they are that. In theory, the trout aren't supposed to see the line anyway, or, if they do, they're not supposed to know what it is, and so the color should not be a problem. I've never met anyone who thought that the color of a floating line really meant anything in particular, though there may be such people. I assume color is just a matter of taste. Sinking lines, on the other hand, are designed to work in the gloomy depths, and so they tend to be drab. There, a garish color could frighten the fish.

A Word or Two About Backing

Here's the situation: You are after big fish, and you hook one. So far, so good. And the better the fish, the more likely he will be to take the fly and run off downstream for a hundred yards or more before the effort of pulling all that line discourages him. But the average fly line is only about thirty yards long. If it were any longer, we would need a reel the size of a wheel rim to hold it, since fly line is as thick as pasta. A reel that size would make casting almost impossible, since the heavy reel would throw the entire rig completely out of balance. And so we encounter a problem—we need lots of line in order to catch big fish, but we cannot make a reel big enough to hold all that line.

The solution to this problem is "backing," which is a thinner, braided line that is attached to the rear end of the fly line. This backing spends most of its time wound tightly on the reel, since smaller trout can be caught quite easily without letting very much line off the reel. But the backing comes into play when a big fish takes the fly and then streaks off downstream or across the river—and just keeps going. The fly line pays out off the reel, the reel sings out in a high C, and the fish runs and runs until suddenly he is "into the backing." He has pulled all the fly line off the reel, but he is still going, and the angler now sees the thinner backing being stripped off the reel. Eventually the weight of the line—both fly line and backing—plus the effort of the run will tire the fish and the angler will be able to start reeling him back, unless the fish manages to break off. (Perhaps there was a wind knot in the leader.) But even in that case the angler will at least have had the thrill of a fish taking him into the backing—always the hallmark of a good hookup and fight.

The breaking strength of most backing for trout fishing is usually around eighteen or twenty pounds, so there's no real worry about it, even though it looks remarkably thin when compared to the fly line.

How much backing you need depends to a large extent on the type of fish you are going after. People who fly fish for bonefish are well advised to have a couple of hundred yards of backing, because these fish run far and fast. People fishing for large salmonids—steelhead and salmon—will also use large rods and heavy lines with plenty of backing. On the other hand, if you are going after smaller brookies in small mountain streams, the odds are that you will be using a light rod and line and that, regardless of how many fish you hook, you will never see the backing. Then again, you never know.

The Reel

The stereotypical Englishman, if we are to believe the books and movies, will often say things like: "Jolly good, what?" I don't know any Englishmen who actually talk like that, but there may be some around. The curious thing about that way of speaking is that addition of the "what?" at the end of a phrase. It adds nothing, makes no sense. I used to wonder about that until I read or heard the following explanation. It seems that when King George III was in the latter stages of insanity, he used to hear voices, but these voices didn't always make themselves clear to George, and he often had to ask for clarification—"What?" These voices intruded themselves at all hours, during lunch or conferences or state dinners or galas. The king might be conducting a meeting with his ministers and, in the middle of a sentence, some spectral voice would murmur to him and he would interrupt his thought to ask: "What?" Style setters and court hangers-on began to notice this habit of speech, and since royalty—however otherwise insane and incompetent—can do no wrong when it comes to fashion, people began to adopt the king's manner of speaking.

It may be that none of this is true, but it makes a good story, what? And we should not be too hard on George, for he was a nature lover of sorts and therefore a kindred spirit. It was George, after all, who knighted an oak tree he admired and also promoted his horse to the rank of general. And while this is not a good advertisement for monarchy as a system of government, it does demonstrate a genuine love of the outdoors.

Speaking of "what," what does George III have to do with reels? Not much, except that the story does illustrate that fashion often causes people to do things that, when viewed from an impartial perspective, make no sense. Consider, for example, the right-handed retrieve on a fly reel. Most people are right handed. This we know. It would follow, then, that most people have a stronger right hand than left, and that most people would therefore want to use their right hand when fighting a fish, i.e., keep their right hand on the rod grip and use the left hand for cranking on the reel. And yet, many people do exactly the opposite. They cast right handed, strike right handed, hold the rod high using the right hand while they strip in excess fly line with their left hand and then, *in the middle of the fight,* they shift the rod to their left hand and start winding on the reel with their right hand to take up the slack. Their reel crank, in other words, is on the right side of the reel and they must therefore use their right hand to crank. This seems odd, you will agree, since all good modern fly reels can be set up to wind with either the right hand or the left hand—it is a simple adjustment of the internal workings of the reel. Why would any right-handed person want his tackle set up so that it required him to switch hands in the middle of a fish fight in order to crank the reel? Why not set up the reel with the crank on the left side so that a right-handed angler can hold the rod in his right hand and reel in the fish with his left?

The answer to this mystery may be—fashion. I have heard it said that one of the Princes of Wales—I think it was Edward, the tubby one who was Victoria's son and heir—liked outdoor sports almost as much as he liked rich foods. He particularly liked to fish. What's more, he was left handed. He therefore did the logical thing and set up his reel to crank with the right hand. Others in his entourage followed suit, even though many of them were right handed. A tradition was born. Here again, this story may be apocryphal, but it is safe to say, I think, that the right-hand retrieve is a traditional setup that has no basis in logic. Of course, most Americans, after cutting their steak, shift their forks from the left to the right hand before taking a bite, and this habit puzzles Europeans who see it as an extra and unnecessary step in the feeding process. So there is at least some precedent for this hand-switching routine. Not surprisingly, in the U.S. the tendency toward right-handed reels seems to be more pronounced in the more tradition-minded sections of the country, such as the East. Out West the style is more practical, and most right-handed people crank with their left hands so that they can fight the fish with their stronger hand. They still switch forks from one hand to the other, however.

The other explanation of the hand-switching routine could be that the old reels were made to be cranked only with the right hand. As an explanation, that has plausibility but no personality, and so I prefer the one about the pudgy prince.

Fly reels are like umpires or secret agents—you want them to do their jobs without drawing attention to themselves, and you don't want them to make any mistakes. They are integral to the game, but they are performing at their best when they go pretty much unnoticed. It used to be customary to observe that fly reels were really just places to store the line, and that may still be true if the angler is only after juvenile brookies in some trickle of a mountain stream. In those cases the angler can get along nicely without really worrying about the reel, since when he hooks a fish, he can simply strip in line with his left hand, secure in the knowledge that the fish is not big enough to dash away or even, in most cases, to break the leader. But when an angler hooks a bigger fish in bigger water, a couple of things will happen—first, the fish will run, and second, the angler will have no choice but to let him do it, because to try to resist (by clamping down on the line and holding it) will only result in a broken leader. When a big fish wants to run, he will run, and if you want to land him eventually, you will have to let him have his fun first.

So, assuming that you do hook a big fish that is capable of running off with the line and taking you into the backing, what do you want the reel to do for you? The sequence of events in the hook-up is the starting point for the answer. First, the angler makes a few casts, and in doing so he will most likely accumulate some excess fly line in his left hand (or in the bottom of the boat or floating on the surface of the stream). And so, when a good fish decides to eat the fly and then dashes off for the far bank, the angler has some slack in the line that he must manage. The technique here is usually just to hold the line in the left hand and let it pay out through the fingers, offering just enough pressure (by pinching between thumb and forefinger) to allow the line to run out smoothly, so that it doesn't get tangled. Eventually the excess line will be used up, and the fish, who is continuing on his way, deeply annoyed, will now start stripping line off the reel. It is at this point that the angler becomes conscious of the reel. The line is ripping off at a furious pace, and the reel is singing its own version of "zing went the strings of my heart." And the angler, who to this point had given relatively little thought to the reel, suddenly begins to appreciate it anew and to hope that the reel is up to the challenge, for what is needed at this point is a reel that will allow the line and backing to pay out smoothly, without overruns and tangles—and yet at the same time will exert some pressure on the fish, some drag on the line, that will ultimately discourage the fish and yet do so without offering so much resistance that the fish can use it to snap the leader. As in political lobbying, just the right amount of pressure is the key. Too much and the leader will break, too little and the reel will spin so fast that it will seize up into a rat's nest of an overrrun, and the fish will break off.

Once the fish has decided that he has had enough for a while, the angler can then begin to wind the line back in. He may do this with his right hand, if he follows the Edwardian cranking style, or he may be a more practical left-handed winder. In either case, the fish, having rested for a time, may decide to go for another sprint. Usually the fish's first close-up look at the eager angler, who is perhaps managing the rod in one hand and a large net in the other, is enough to send him on one last panicky dash. Here again, the angler has no choice but to let him go. And once again the reel must do its work smoothly. If all goes according to the book, the fish will eventually become tired and give up, at which point the angler can reel him back in, remove the fly and then send him on his way, sadder but wiser.

The reel, in short, is crucial to landing good fish. In fact, the only way to fight a good fish is "on the reel." You really have no choice in the matter, since a good fish will get you on the reel and into the backing before you have much time to think about it. Your job in such a case is to make sure that the slack that may be in the line at the moment of hook-up does not get tangled when the fish makes his first mad dash for freedom and that you get the fish on the reel as soon as possible.

When a fish eats a fly and then runs off with it, the line pays out, and the more line there is in the water, the more difficult it is for the fish to pull it. The action of the current may pull on the line and therefore on the fish. The weight of the line itself becomes harder to drag as more line is exposed. So the fish has a geometrically more difficult task the farther he runs. To make matters worse—for the fish—the reel has "drag" built into it. Drag is mechanical resistance, just like the brakes on a car. As the line pays out, the drag mechanism works against the turning of the reel, and thereby makes the whole process that much tougher for the fish. Drag is adjustable. There is a lever or dial on the side of the reel that allows you to set it to a degree you think is appropriate. Of course, if you set the drag too high, the resistance may be too strong, and the fish might be able to snap the leader on his first dash. The object is to let the fish run, but to tax him for the privilege.

In short, fly reels are often underappreciated, until the time comes for them to go to work. Having lost a good fish once because a reel came apart when the fish made a run, I can attest to the sense of mild disappointment one feels when a reel fails. I can also vouch for the sense of genuine appreciation an angler feels when the reel performs as expected. Or maybe relief is the better word. (I am probably exaggerating here: a good modern fly reel works really well. I've only ever had that one failure, so far.)

Reels are made to hold certain lines. Since a 4-weight line is thinner than, say, an 8-weight, a reel for the former does not need as much capacity and so can be smaller. Moreover, when you are fishing a 4-weight line, your 4-weight rod will be lighter and, perhaps, shorter than a rod designed for a heavier line. That means that the reel should be lighter too, so that the combination is well balanced. Most manufacturers make a series of reels ranging in diameter from two and a half inches to around four inches. The bigger reels naturally hold the heavier lines and more backing. There is no need to have a separate reel for each line weight. Most reel manufacturers offer four or so different reel sizes, since the smallest reel can easily accommodate all line sizes from 1 to 4, while the larger reels can hold several line weights each.

Reels have two basic parts—the spool and the frame. The frame contains the basic reel mechanisms, and the spool holds the line. You can buy extra spools for reels, which means that you can carry different types of line, floating and sinking for example, and when you want to change from one to the other, you can just change spools, i.e., put the new spool on the same reel frame. (Here is another opportunity to spend in the name of economy.)

Fly reels come in single- and double-action (or multiplying) models, like six-shooters. Single action means that when you wind the handle through one complete revolution, you get one complete turn of the spool. Double action means that you get more than one revolution of the spool with each turn of the handle. Most fly reels used in trout fishing are single-action models. Some manufacturers have even made automatic reels—reels that do not require cranking, but operate by pressing levers, or something. These are completely beyond the pale; the less said about them, the better.

Modern fly reels look a lot like antique fly reels. They are sleeker and more mechanically sophisticated, but in general the design hasn't changed, at least outwardly, all that much over the last century. That seems to me to be an additional virtue. And they have a beauty all their own, I think, especially when attached to their partner in the game, the fly rod. In form, the two are opposites—the rod thin and long, the reel round and sturdy. Don Quixote and Sancho Panza. And together they make a combination that is not only useful but also aesthetically appealing. They are the straight line and the circle, the two basic elements of all design, which may be why there are so many rods and reels hanging on the walls of country inns and taverns around the world. People like to look at them. They just go well together.

The Rod

First a word on rods and poles. While there are such things as fishing poles, there is no such thing as a fly pole. They are fly rods. To call a rod a pole is the same as calling a ship, like the QE II, a boat. This is a semantic quibble, of course, and there may be just a whiff of snobbery about it. But it is one of those distinctions that seems to matter, and to hear a rod called a pole is like hearing someone say "just between you and I"—it clanks rudely against the ear. Politeness precludes our saying something about prepositions requiring the objective case; nor would we correct someone who characterized a rod as a pole. But these are regrettable solecisms, nonetheless. Huck Finn would carry a fishing pole, but Huck was after catfish and other such watery democrats with a worm. If you were after catfish with a worm, you would want a fishing pole too, something long, gnarled, and reel-less. Tie a bobber on the line, and you'd have the ultimate populist catfish rig. But when you're after trout with a fly, you're using a rod. (Here ends the editorial.)

We know that rods are categorized by line weights; 4-weight rods are designed for 4-weight lines, 5-weights for 5-weight lines, and so on. Good manufacturers are careful about their engineering. That means that while you can generally go up or down one line weight, you will most likely get optimal performance from the rod if you use the line weight it was designed for. You can probably put a 6-weight line on a 7-weight rod and cast it without embarrassment. But the rod's action will probably not be as efficient as it would be with the 7-weight line it was intended for. At least, so the rod manufacturers tell us. On the other hand, I know some guides who use a particular kind of 7-weight rod with a 6-weight line—but only a double-taper 6 weight; they claim it gives better performance than a 7-weight, weight-forward line. (If you are a novice and you understand that sentence, you have come a long way.) This level of discourse is probably a lot higher than most of us care to go. But it shows that fly fishing offers nearly infinite opportunities for discussion and debate and that it puts other, simpler pastimes—such as, say, golf—totally in the shade when it comes to esoterica.

This is not a gratuitous slap at golf, but merely a matter of obvious truth. Although most anglers would agree with Mark Twain that golf is "a good walk, spoiled," we do not begrudge its practitioners their innocent pleasures. Besides, it keeps them off the streams.

Fly rods generally weigh somewhere between two and five ounces, and the heavier the line that the rod is designed to throw, the heavier the rod, as a general rule. But these days, most people don't pay too much attention to the physical weight of the rod, since modern materials (such as graphite) allow rods to be both lighter and stronger than the materials our ancestors used. Instead, people who are shopping for a rod focus on length and line weight.

The length of the rod can vary regardless of line weight. While the heavier weight (line weight, not actual weight) rods tend to be somewhat longer—anywhere from eight to ten feet—the length of lighter rods can vary pretty sharply. I have a seven foot, 4-weight rod and a nine foot, 4-weight. (As I said earlier, rods do proliferate.) The reverse is not true, however: you would not expect to see a seven-foot rod designed to throw a 9-weight line. It would be considered too short to cast the heavier line. The typical length of a 9-weight rod would be nine feet or more. At the opposite extreme, I have seen a six-foot rod designed for a 1-weight line. This toothpick is more in the category of novelty, but if you were fishing in a small stream for six-inch trout or in a farm pond for bluegills, it would probably be a lot of fun. So, while there is some correlation between rod length and line weight, it is very rough. If we return to the mythical angler who only ever wants one rod, we would probably advise him to select a 6-weight rod of eight and a half or nine feet.

The object of fly-rod design is to get a match between the material and dimensions of the rod and the degree of flex required to propel a certain weight of fly line. You could cast a fly line with a broomstick, but you couldn't cast it very far or very accurately. Modern fly rods are constructed of essentially three different types of materials, each offering slightly different characteristics, but all having the essential attribute, the *sine qua non*—the ability to flex *and* the ability to spring back once flexed. After all, you can flex a piece of licorice, but you would not expect it to spring back into its original shape. It has flexibility but no stiffness, no ability to spring back.

The great breakthrough of the last two decades or so has been the development of the graphite rod. Graphite has greater strength and stiffness (the ability to spring back when flexed) yet is lighter than any other rod material. That means that graphite rods are both more powerful and easier to use than rods of other materials. Graphite rods are constructed by wrapping strips of paper-thin carbonized fiber around a tapered, dowel-like device called a mandrel and then removing the mandrel, so that the interior of a graphite rod is hollow almost up to the thinnest section, the tip. Graphite's primary advantages are that it is both light and strong, and it is the stiffest of all the rod materials. It not only flexes well; it springs back powerfully.

The other primary rod material is bamboo, also called cane. Bamboo rods are made by stripping the outside sections of a piece of bamboo. These strips are cut and shaped so that when they are viewed from the end they look like triangles. The strips are then tapered, so that the rod sections grow thinner as they near the tip. Five or six tapered strips are then glued together, so that the finished rod when viewed from the end looks like a pentagon or a hexagon, and the rod is solid to the core, since all the points of the tapered pieces meet at the center. The key thing about this kind of rod manufacture, as compared to the graphite, is that it is done mostly by hand. It is therefore more expensive, often by about a factor of ten. If you pay two hundred dollars for a graphite rod, you can pay two thousand for bamboo. Antique bamboo rods are now sought by collectors, who are driving the price of these rods so high that people no longer use the rods; they just display them. Fair enough, since they are minor works of art, and major works of craftsmanship. But you can still buy new bamboo rods at a price that, while high, is within reach of most serious fly fishermen. It may mean going without other essentials for a while, but all decisions involve compromise.

What's the difference between graphite and bamboo, aside from price? Aesthetics don't enter into this question too aggressively, since the really good graphite rod is every bit as lovely in its own way as the bamboo rod. They are different looking, though, for graphite does have a space-age cachet, whereas bamboo definitely looks to be from a slower-paced era. But each has much to recommend it when it comes to the question of looks. No, aside from price, the real difference is in the action of the rod. Bamboo is widely regarded as being "slower" than graphite. This means in essence that the rod has a different feel, a softer, longer-flexing character. Bamboo rods tend to flex nearly down to the rod handle. Graphite on the other hand is faster; it flexes only part way down the rod—just the tip, the upper section of the rod, flexes. As a rule, this kind of action generates more line speed. This additional power and faster action means that the caster can throw a tighter loop, and that in turn means greater distance and better accuracy into the wind. Still, some people prefer the slower action of bamboo, not only because it is the traditional rod material but also because it feels comfortable. The only way to evaluate this difference is to cast both kinds of rods and to see which you prefer.

If you are like many anglers you will, over time, acquire one bamboo rod and several graphite rods, and you will use the graphite rods much more often than the bamboo. The bamboo will be like the '56 Jaguar that you have (metaphorically speaking) in your garage, the one that comes out only on clear days in the summer. (The good news is that the bamboo rod will actually perform, whereas the '56 Jag probably will not start.) The graphite rods, on the other hand, are the BMW's—sleek, functional, pricey, but generally worth it.

But what of the Fords and Chevys? There is an equivalent—fiberglass. Fiberglass rods are inexpensive and available in the usual line weights. The may lack a certain *je ne sais quoi* in the beauty category, but they will not cause widespread revulsion among your fishing buddies when you pull them out of their rod sacks. And the simple fact is, they work fine. If you can cast, you can cast a fiberglass rod. If you cannot cast, bamboo and graphite will not do it for you. (It is true, however, that graphite is the most forgiving material. It is, in that sense, like one of the new oversize tennis rackets that has a big sweet spot which compensates for minor errors in technique. Not surprisingly, many of these new rackets are graphite, too.)

In short, if you want to get into fly fishing without spending next month's rent, fiberglass is a good place to start. The rods may lack some of the power of graphite and much of the feel of bamboo, but they can get the job done. The differences are all at the margin, as they say in politics, and a novice would not recognize them. Further, even an experienced angler on a budget may conclude that it is more fun to have several different fiberglass rods than just one expensive rod.

All rods, regardless of the material they're made of, have the same basic attachments and features. First, there are the guides. These are the loops through which we feed the line. These are not "eyes," by the way, and to refer to them this way is another of those minor *faux pas* that one tries to avoid. The guides are attached to the rod by countless turns of thread which are then varnished or epoxied to create a smooth and attractive finish. It is possible to wear out a set of guides—the action of the line going through cast after cast gradually wears the metal away. One of your goals should therefore be to wear out the guides on your favorite rod, because it takes a lot of fishing to do it.

Second, there are the ferrules. Most rods come in sections—either two or three pieces are the most common, although some manufacturers make four- and five piece rods designed for people who travel and never want to be without their rods. Ferrules are male/female joints that connect the various sections of the rod. Most people use the term ferrule to refer to both sexes, that is, both halves of the joint. By definition, a one-piece rod has no ferrules. And there are one-piece rods made, especially for saltwater game-fish, since some people believe that joints in the rod weaken or adversely affect the action of the rod, or both. This is probably not true of the graphite rods, but here again opinions vary.

As you use a rod throughout a day's angling, the action of casting may gradually loosen the connection; that is, the tip of the rod may slide out of the ferrule. It is a strange feeling to be casting and to have the upper half of your rod suddenly fall out. You think you have broken the rod, and then you think that the tip, which is most likely in the water, will sink and be lost forever. But of course the tip is still attached to the line, or vice versa, and you only need to retrieve the one to get the other. Such embarrassing moments can be avoided by occasionally checking to make sure the two (or three) sections of the rod are still firmly joined together.

Third, there is the grip, which is generally made of cork. There are several different shapes of grip, and here again the shape is entirely a matter of personal preference. My own preference in this area is so uninformed that I don't think I could really tell you what sort of grips my various rods have. I just use them as they are. Other people have more well-formed opinions on grips, I am sure, and if it didn't matter, rod manufacturers probably would not go to the trouble of offering different grip shapes. So, here again, you need to try different kinds and see what suits.

And finally there is the reel seat. You will not be astonished to learn that this is where the reel is attached. Once again there are several different setups available, and none makes much difference as far as I am able to determine.

And that pretty much covers the basic terminology of the rod.

Different rods, especially rods designed for heavier weights, may have additional features, such as a screw-in "fighting butt," which is an extension to the handle that you can jam into your gut when fighting a tarpon or some such salty heavyweight. Fighting butts are not used on trout rods, as a rule. You can beat most trout without any help.

One last point about rods—they will break. They will break when fighting a fish, sometimes. But more likely they will break when you slam them in the car door or step on them or pull them awkwardly out of the rod tube or do a hundred other things that you immediately regret. Some manufacturers guarantee their rods even when they are broken through carelessness. Such guarantees are worth having, even though as a general rule you can fish for decades with a good graphite rod as long as you are careful with it around screen doors and such. Of course, you may have to replace the guides every so many years, but that's all to the good.

So, the basic setup has four elements—leader, line, reel, and rod. The question now becomes: What do we do with them?

Casting

*Can't hear with a bawk of bats, all thim liffeying
waters of. Ho, talk save us! My foos won't moos.*
—James Joyce, *Finnegan's Wake*

THERE'S SUCH A THING AS ARTISTIC LICENSE, a conscious violation of everyday rules. James Joyce, for example, didn't actually talk like that. He knew the laws of English grammar and spelling, and in the normal course of business and socializing he was able to make himself understood. But when he picked up a pen he bent the rules, and was satisfied. Similarly, most modern artists who paint abstractions can draw a reasonable likeness of a human body or a bowl of peaches or whatever. They just don't want to. And jazz musicians can play a melody, but they think it's more fun to use the score only as a sort of distant reference point; they'd rather improvise, and the result, as Twain said about Wagner's

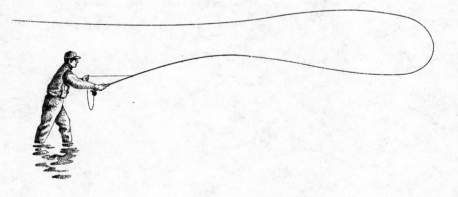

music, isn't as bad as it sounds. All artists start with a basic set of rules, master them, and then adapt them, sometimes beyond recognition, to their own personal tastes. They develop their own style. Same with casting. You will see some really good casters who don't seem to be following the rules and who in fact seem to be violating them with impunity. But in fact, every good caster is following the one key rule—*Let it load*. Individuals may adapt their wrist action or the angle of the rod or the angle of their elbow and so on, but every good fly caster is letting the rod do the work.

Let it load. Okay. But exactly what does that mean? The answer lies in the basic mechanics of the cast.

THE MECHANICS

We are all born with the ability to cast badly. The greater our inexperience, the more interesting are the tangles and muddles we can create with rod and line. If this is true, and it is, it implies that casting technique is not natural. It is especially unnatural to grown-

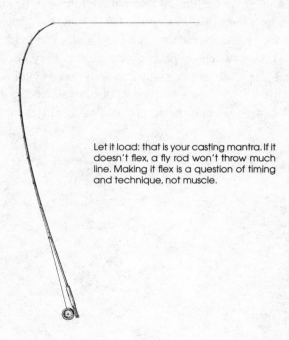

Let it load: that is your casting mantra. If it doesn't flex, a fly rod won't throw much line. Making it flex is a question of timing and technique, not muscle.

up boys who have been throwing things—rocks, balls, paper wads—since they were first able to toddle. And as women have become more and more involved in organized athletics, they too have begun throwing earlier and earlier. The phrase "throws like a girl" may soon be as obsolete as a horsehair fly line. I will go even further and say that men and women are equally incompetent when they first pick up a fly rod. Our ineptitude stems from a lack of technique, certainly, but it also comes from a misunderstanding of the idea of casting. It is not throwing. Strength has very little to do with it. Women bodybuilders feverishly pumping iron are making a mistake if their goal is to improve their fly casting. These oiled Amazons have no advantage over a pale and elderly librarian who has just a nodding acquaintance with physical activity and whose only knowledge of muscle tone comes from romantic novels. And the same goes for men. If any of those burly Russian weightlifters with bulging muscles and bulging eyes were to pick up a fly rod for the first time, he would produce a rat's nest of line that not even a starving whitefish would look at.

The confusion (or misdirected effort) results from the fact that the rod does the work of casting, though most people don't believe this at first. The more effort we put into it, the more we try to impose our will, the less likely we are to succeed. Like the wrestler who tries to out-muscle a judo master, we find that our strength can work against us. "Less," as the poet Browning observed, "is more"—at least in terms of the physical effort in casting. This may seem contradictory at first. But once we've digested the basic theory of casting, it all comes together, with a little practice. This is not to say that strength doesn't play any part in casting, but rather that it is not everything. The key is proper technique, technique which controls the physical strength of the caster, and applies it at the proper moment in the proper amount.

You will remember that the art of fly casting consists of throwing the line rather than the fly. The line's weight flexes the rod and gives it power. This flexing happens twice, actually, and you should think of the cast as having two separate but equal steps: the backcast and the forward cast. The backcast starts the process. Assume that the line is lying on the water, as straight as a Marine's crease. The weight of the line and the resistance of the water—the friction of the surface tension—combine to resist your effort to pick up the line. You raise your arm, the line resists, and the rod bends. This flexing of the rod has to be sufficiently forceful to launch the line over your head, where it then pays out slowly until it's almost horizontal to the ground behind you, and you can feel it flexing the rod back. At that point you start the forward cast so that the action of your arm going forward counteracts the weight of the line stretching out behind you and therefore flexes the rod even more and creates the power you need to shoot the line toward the target. This action creates the casting loop, and at the end of the exercise the leader turns over and the fly lands delicately on the surface, whereupon you feel a pleasure far out of proportion to the real merits of the accomplishment.

Easier said than done, you might be thinking. Well, yes, as in most things. But it's not all *that* difficult. It's just a matter of acquiring the stroke. Remember Norman Maclean and his metronome? He was trying to describe the stroke, but where he went off the rails was in describing the stroke as a two-o'clock–ten-o'clock motion. Actually, the motion is more a nine-o'clock–twelve-o'clock–nine-o'clock motion with a brief stop at ten o'clock on the forward cast. That sentence may be confusing, so perhaps a better way to describe the stroke is to break it down into its component parts:

> (1) Start with your rod pointed at the water, the tip almost touching the surface. Strip in any slack that might be in the line. This extra line will fall onto the surface or into the bottom of the boat, but no matter. Assuming that you are right-handed, pinch the line between the thumb and forefinger of your left hand; position your left hand about twelve inches from your right.

(2) Keep your wrist stiff and your elbow stationary, as though the upper part of your sleeve were sewn loosely to the side of your shirt. (Old-time casting instructors used to tell you to imagine holding a Bible or a gin bottle—depending on their habits—between your elbow and ribcage.)

(3) Lift the rod firmly, but keep your elbow relatively fixed next to your side. The elbow acts as the hinge. This action will throw the line up and over your head. There is no room for tentativeness here. The backcast should be vigorous. If it's not, the fly is apt to land in your shirt instead of sailing over your head. Keep your wrist stiff. A limp wrist has no more place in fly casting than it does at a convention of Harley-Davidson enthusiasts. You still have the line pinched between your left thumb and forefinger; if you let it go or let it slip, you'll create slack that will ruin the cast, because the line will not be able to flex the rod. Your left hand should move in concert with your right; in other words, as the right hand raises the rod tip, the left should follow in roughly the same plane.

(4) Stop the rod at about twelve o'clock—that is, stop the backcast when the rod tip is pointed straight up. There's obviously room for error here; precision is not the object. The point is to stop the rod when it is essentially vertical.

(5) Let the line straighten out behind you until you feel it beginning to flex the upright rod. The reason you stop the rod at twelve o'clock is to create maximum resistance to the line as it pays out behind you, creating the optimal angle for the line to flex the rod. If you were to let the rod drift backwards over your shoulder, dropping

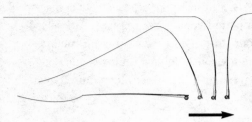

The backcast begins with a tight line, accelerates smoothly and rapidly, and stops sharply as the rod passes the vertical, allowing the line to roll out behind you.

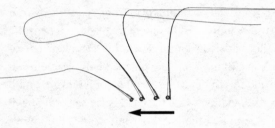

More push than snap, the forward cast accelerates through a fairly narrow arc before stopping sharply. As the line unrolls toward the target, you may lower the rod until it's horizontal.

off from the vertical, the line's ability to bend the rod backwards would be diminished. Don't let the line slip from your left thumb and forefinger.

(6) Wait for the line to pay out behind you. It is not considered cheating to turn your head and look. Even the best casters do it now and then. This waiting is the key. Remember the pole vaulter with the fiberglass pole—he waits until the pole is fully loaded with power before starting his movement over the bar. Timing is the key, not strength.

(7) When you feel the rod being flexed backwards, begin your forward cast. Keep your elbow where it was—next to your ribcage—and bring your forearm forward. Keep your wrist stiff, as though you were wearing a cast. A stiff wrist prevents you from inadvertently releasing any of the energy in the flexed rod. This forward cast creates the shooting loop that flies over your head toward the target. Don't let go of the line in your left hand.

(8) On the forward cast, stop the rod at about ten o'clock. (Assume that the surface of the water represents nine o'clock.) Stopping the rod at this point allows the line to pay out smoothly in front of you. The loop unfolds gradually, so that at the end of the cast the line and leader have straightened out. If you want to "shoot" the line, you can let the line pull free from your left hand at this point. The power of the forward moving loop will pull extra line from the slack you were managing with your left hand. If you're comfortable with the amount of line you have in the air, and don't want to shoot any additional line, keep your left forefinger and thumb clamped on the line.

(9) When the line and leader have straightened, let the rod tip drift down to the horizontal (nine o'clock), and the line and leader will fall softly to the surface without arousing the notice of even the most watchful and skittish of trout.

(10) Congratulate yourself on an artful cast.

That's it. It seems simple enough: buy a good rod and stay out of its way. Let it do its job. "Empower" the rod by using a good stroke and let it do the rest. What could possibly go wrong with this process?

Plenty. The question before the house is—why?

We can start to answer that question by reiterating the fact that all novice fly fishermen automatically know how to cast poorly. Our repertoire of inept casts is comprehensive. Sometimes the line does one thing, sometimes it does another. Occasionally it seems to have a life of its own. Often it seems to aim itself at our persons with malicious intent. But in all of these misadventures there is a symptom of what's wrong; there are clues in the chaos. By recognizing these clues, we can make the necessary adjustments and improve our offerings. What follows is a (partial) listing of classically tragic casts—tragic in the sense that they cause a sense of fear and pity in anyone who happens to be watching (such as a nervous fishing guide). Perhaps by examining these fatal flaws, we can learn to avoid them.

The Toscanini

A rod is not a baton. The more you wave it around, the less harmony you achieve. Most orchestra conductors start the proceedings with their batons pointed straight up. Casters should start with the rod pointed down, at the water. If the rod is pointed straight up, there must necessarily be slack in the line; much of it will be gathered at your feet. This slack means that when you start the backcast there will be virtually no resistance from the line, and the rod therefore will not flex sufficiently. No backcast, no forward cast.

The best stroke operates in a single plane. Back, stop, forward. If we wave the rod around in different planes, the line flies in different directions. The result is a lessening of the line's force on the backcast and a consequent lessening of its ability to flex the rod.

Of course, even if your rod is pointed at the surface of the water, you won't be able to generate much power in your backcast if your line is gathered in a pile or has so much slack in it that when you start the backcast the line can't offer any resistance. When your line is relatively straight and your rod is pointed down at the surface of the water, your backcast starts to flex the rod from the very start of the motion, and you achieve full power from the start, just like flooring a Ferrari. If there's slack in your line at the start, it's more like flooring a six-cylinder '63 Falcon—the results are unimpressive. So strip in any slack before you start the backcast.

The Limp Wrist

You cast primarily with your forearm and elbow. Your wrist has very little to do with the process. In fact, when the wrist gets involved, it generally makes a hash of things. Consider the process: you lift the line off the water and in so doing flex the rod. This initial flex gives the rod the power to propel the line over your head so that it pays out behind. You stop the rod at about twelve o'clock because you want the line paying out behind to pull at a ninety-degree angle to the rod in order to flex the rod to the optimum. Now, if at that precise moment when the line starts to pull back on the rod and flex it, you "break your wrist," as we used to say in baseball, the pull of the line will not flex the rod. When you try to come forward with your cast, no power is available in the rod to propel the line, and the cast most likely will collapse.

To clarify this concept, imagine you wanted to build a primitive catapult. You get a springy piece of wood about six feet long, sharpen one end, and pound that end into the ground. Then you tie a sling to the other end. When all is ready, you put a rock in the sling and start pulling back on the whole rig. The stick bends backward, ever backward, until it's flexed to the maximum and therefore fully loaded with power. If at that moment, just when you're ready to let go, the other end of the stick comes loose from the ground, what will happen? The whole effort will collapse. That's what happens when you let your wrist bend at the top of your cast.

The problem occurs because at the moment the fly rod is fully bent and loaded with power, the operator does something that lets the energy (contained in the flex) escape. In short, the wrist shouldn't really play a role. That is the primary difference between casting and throwing. A pitcher uses all the joints in his arm—shoulder, elbow, wrist. A caster only uses shoulder and elbow. The wrist should be locked so that it's an extension of the rod grip. You stop the rod when it's vertical in order to load it with power. If you let the line drag your wrist backwards, the rod stops flexing, and the cast is ruined.

It's also possible, though more difficult, to unload the rod with your elbow. If, for example, you cast by bringing your elbow up next to your ear so that your forearm is parallel to the water and the rod is pointing down at the surface behind you, there will be no flex. The chances are good that when you make your forward cast the line and fly will travel straight up and then straight down and land on your hat.

The Blacksmith

People who remember the 1960s might recall a tune called "If I Had a Hammer." It was performed earnestly by a number of earnest folk singers and then later, less earnestly, by a rock singer. Some of these would-be Vulcans have apparently taken up fly fishing, for you can spot them by their distinctive casting technique as they muscle their forward cast from the perpendicular straight down to the water without ever pausing to let the line and leader catch up. It's one smooth hammer blow. The result is that the line hits the water first—the part of the line closest to the rod tip—while the rest of the line rolls out onto the surface like a wave breaking on the beach. The bottom half of the loop, instead of being in the air, is actually on the water, while the top half of the loop is still flying forward. As a result, the last things to land on the surface of the water are the leader and the fly. This is not the end of the world, but it's not a very elegant way to present the fly. More importantly, the line rolling along the surface of the water could disturb a skittish trout, and will certainly disturb any other trout that might be lying between you and the one you're after. Further, sometimes the loop collapses before it unfurls completely, and the result is a tangle on the water somewhere between caster and target.

You can avoid this unhappy situation by stopping the rod on the forward cast at about ten o'clock to let the line to catch up, allowing the loop to unfurl gradually. Then, when the line and leader, while still airborne, have completely straightened out in front, let the rod tip drop down to nine o'clock as the line and leader drift down to the surface.

The Pasta Special

Nothing delights the heart of a hungry angler so much as a plate of pasta and, perhaps, a beaker of something red. But only at dinner. To turn a fly line and leader into a still-life without clam sauce is deeply unsatisfying. These trattorian tangles generally result from a weak forward cast. The caster lifts the line off the water smartly, lets it pay out behind, and then, at the moment of maximum backward flex, fails to apply enough strength to the forward cast. As a result, the line and leader collapse somewhere overhead and fall to the water in a heap. The loop collapses because the caster does not apply enough power.

These tangles can also result from stopping the rod too soon on the forward cast, say at eleven o'clock. The power is interrupted, and the loop collapses, often just overhead.

The Rawhide

At the time of this writing, my son is a college student during the school months and a fly-fishing guide in Idaho during the summers, an insufferable combination that leaves me green with envy. Worse yet, when we fish together and, on those rare occasions when I happen to snap the fly on the backcast, I hear a derisive "EEE-HAW—Rawhide!" This lamentable lack of filial respect occurs whenever I rush the forward cast and thereby "crack the whip." Those men who remember snapping wet towels at their teammates in the locker room understand this phenomenon. (In the interest of fairness, I should not assume that women do not also snap towels in the locker room. Perhaps they do.) This snapping happens because, while the fly and the leader are still traveling backward, the caster rushes the forward cast. He starts it too early, and as a result accelerates the final few feet that the leader and fly travel. The whip cracks. You can hear it, and you can sometimes see the results, for if you look behind you may see the snapped-off fly drifting down onto the surface of the stream and then floating away with the current. When you hear that snapping sound, it means you're rushing your forward cast. Remember the pole vaulter and wait, wait, wait. Let it load.

On the other hand, waiting *too* long can also create problems, such as...

The Turtle Snapper

A snapping turtle is one thing; snapping a turtle is something else. A turtle complacently swimming across the stream, his head jutting above the surface, may be surprised by sudden splashes around his head as though some small boy were potting at him with a BB gun. But no, it's a fly hitting the surface with every backcast, for the caster has let the line drift too far down before starting the forward cast. Just as gravity takes its toll on the physiques of humans, it also affects a fly line. This is not an irrecoverable disaster, but consider the flight of the fly as it comes forward after having touched down on the water—its trajectory must necessarily be lower at first. And as it flies forward, instead of clearing your head and torso, as it would with a decent cast, it flies toward you, apparently bent on revenge for some unspecified wrong. Or, if you can manage to clear your person with the forward cast, the trajectory of the line must necessarily be parabolic; that is, the fly starts at the surface behind you, climbs in an arc over your head, and then lands heavily on the water in front. You may have escaped being punctured, but the presentation of the fly is damp and messy. (According to some casting instructiors, the drooping loop resulting from the delayed forward cast is also a primary cause of wind knots.)

The answer here is simple—don't let the line fall below the horizontal on the backcast. This may sound like telling a fat person to eat less, but it's actually useful advice, for all the caster needs to do is turn around and watch the backcast in order to know when to start the forward cast.

The Shirtfront

A weak backcast will not lift the line over your head, but it will lift it into your face and front. This may only result in your having the chance to chew on some fly line. Or it may result in having a fly stuck somewhere in cloth or flesh. There are two things to remember. First, a vigorous backcast is the key to starting a good cast. If you lift the line smartly from the water, and if there's no slack in the line when you start, the line will fly harmlessly over your head. Second, you must always wear glasses when you're fly fishing. In fact, it's a good rule never to be around a line and hook of any description—fly, spinner, bait, whatever—without protective glasses. I cringe every time I see a TV commercial with some actor blithely casting, usually badly, without glasses. And those heart-warming scenes of little children learning to fish on Saturday-morning fishing shows are accidents waiting to happen, because invariably the kids are not wearing glasses. Regardless of how proficient you are with a fly rod, occasionally the line will do something unexpected. Wind, for example, can overcome the best technique and send the line flying wildly. Anyone who fishes without wearing glasses is running the risk of losing an eye.

SLACK LINES, TIGHT LINES, AND FINGERING

There are many big questions that continually pose themselves to philosophers and ordinary intellects alike. What is the nature of reality? Is there life on other planets? Is slack in a fly line a good thing or bad?

As with many such questions, the answer, as far as slack is concerned, is "It depends." If you have a recalcitrant dog on a tight leash, when you pull the leash the dog will move. If, on the other hand, there are loops of slack in the leash, when you tug, the dog will not feel it. The slack absorbs your pull. This same principle applies both in casting and managing the line once it's on the water. Slack in the line when you start to cast means the line will not be able to flex the rod and the cast will therefore fail. Slack in the line once it's on the water means you'll have difficulty setting the hook in the event that a fish takes the fly, because when you lift the rod tip to set the hook, the slack absorbs the strike, and the fly doesn't move. If the fly doesn't move, the hook cannot penetrate, and the fish, having realized the error of his ways, spits out the fly and goes on his way. The lesson, therefore, is that tight lines mean effective striking.

On the other hand, slack is sometimes desirable. In some cases—many cases, in fact—you need to throw some slack into a line as it floats on the surface of the water. This slack helps to prevent the line and fly from dragging. In other words, a tight line thrown across the current will immediately be swept away, and the fly will therefore drag sideways across the stream instead of floating naturally with the current. You reduce this drag by throwing some slack in the line. The slack, in effect, absorbs the effects of the current for a time and allows the fly to float in the same direction and at the same speed as the current. The fly matches the motion of a natural insect. Generally, you throw this slack upstream of the fly. (This is called mending the line, on which more later.) Of course, if a fish takes the fly, the slack makes it harder to set the hook. But that just requires a more vigorous strike. It's more difficult, but it can be done. And without this mending, it's unlikely that any fish will accept your offerings. (Trout will sometimes take a dragging fly, but they're not supposed to, and most of them know it.)

So the lesson is that slack is sometimes agreeable, sometimes not. As with an adolescent child, the question is one of management—managing the line in order to create slack when we want it and eliminate it when we don't. Which brings us to the subject of hands and, more specifically, fingers.

Let's consider a situation in which you don't want slack, such as when you're wading and casting upstream. You know this is a good tactic, since the fish are also facing upstream, so you cast a fly above them and let it drift down to them. There's no real problem with drag in this situation, because the line is cast directly upstream instead of across the current. Your problem therefore is with the line floating back to you. It tends to gather around your feet rather quickly, and that amount of slack in the line makes striking difficult. What to do?

Strip it in. Stripping the line is a technique of gathering up the slack, so that when a fish takes, you can strike effectively. Assume that you're a right-handed caster, you've made a good cast, and the fly is floating in the current, searching for a fish and coming straight back to you. The line, also borne by the current, is gathering in loops in front of you. Your rod is pointed more or less at the surface, your right hand is on the grip, just above the reel, and your right index finger is over the line, holding the line loosely against the rod grip. Meanwhile, your left hand is pulling in the slack. Most likely you're using your thumb and forefinger to do this, though there are no rules against using other digits, too. Most anglers simply let the loop of slack drop into the stream and float out behind, but some like to gather it in a lasso arrangement in their left hand as they strip. All the while, your right index finger is still pressing the line gently against the rod grip. This is the tried-and-true position for the right index finger whenever the line is on the water. That way, if a fish strikes, you can clamp down with your finger to bind the line against the grip while you raise the rod tip to set the hook.

When it's time to cast again, your line is relatively short because you've stripped in all of the extra line. Therefore, little, if any slack is in the line on the water, and you can make an effective backcast using the technique already discussed. In other words, you lift the backcast, hold tight with the left thumb and forefinger in order to maintain a slackless backcast, throw a couple of false casts in order to work out the line that had gathered around your feet, and start the whole thing again.

"But hold on," you might be saying, "what's all this about false casts? I thought you said to avoid false casting. "

I did say that, and I meant it. But I also said that false casting has its uses, and they are, primarily, three.

The first is to help you out of situations such as the one we've been discussing. In other words, as you strip in the line, you gradually shorten the amount of line available for casting (most of it is floating in slack coils at your feet). In order to shake out some additional line from the slack coils, you throw false casts, and with every forward cast you let a little line slide through your left finger and thumb. Then, when you have enough line out, you let the cast fall to the surface.

The second use of false casting is to measure the cast. You may be fishing to a particular fish or to a specific spot. You want to hit it exactly, but you can't tell how much line you'll need. So you make a couple of false casts, and when the fly seems to be above the target, you let it fall to the surface.

The third use of false casting is to help you dry out the fly. Dry flies gradually become soaked as they spend time on the water. A few false casts will "airbrush" the water out of your fly and help it to resume its high profile on the water. (Flotation treatments—powder, liquid, or goop—are the best means of keeping a dry fly floating. Just apply some of this stuff to the fly and it will float like a natural, maybe better. False casting is just a supplemental aid to flotation.)

So, false casting has its uses. But the earlier point about keeping false casts to a minimum still applies. The longer the fly is in the air, the more susceptible the leader is to the attentions of the wind, and the more likely tangles and wind knots are to appear.

Now let's assume that a fish decides to eat the fly. You see the strike, tighten down with your right index finger to lock the line against the rod grip, and raise the rod tip to set the hook. Assuming it's a good fish, it will run, and you'll have to let it go. To do this, you release the line from under your right finger and let the line pay out between your left thumb and index finger until all the slack is gone, and the fish is on the reel, with no slack line anywhere. What's not on the reel is in the water, attached to an angry fish. At this point the reel is zinging and you're wondering whether you have enough backing.

If it turns out not to be such a good fish, then you can simply strip in the excess line with your left hand; there's no need to fight a small fish on the reel. Just keep your right index finger clamped over the line while your left hand strips in the excess line, and the unimpressive fish will follow, reluctantly. But release your right index finger when you hook a fish that will run. How will you know which sort of fish you have? Don't worry, you'll know. It may take the bitter experience of losing a good fish by trying to clamp down and hold him. But after that, you'll know the difference between a fish that needs to run and one that you can just strip in.

In short, the primary function of your left hand is line management—ensuring that there's no slack in the line as it floats on the surface, so you can either set the hook when a fish takes or lift the line smartly for a backcast. The primary function of the right index finger is to keep a tight line in case a fish strikes, so that when you raise the rod tip to set the hook there's no slack in the line, no chance for the fish to spit out the fly.

COPING WITH WIND

The basic mechanics of the cast obtain in all situations, but sometimes circumstances require adjustments in technique. Sometimes you have to cope with wind. Adjustments will also be needed when the fish are not eating on the surface and you want to add some weight to your fly, or when you have to contend with overhanging trees and bushes, or a cliff at your back, or a strong current that can sweep the line away as soon as it touches down. Happily, for every problem created by circumstances, there is a solution, of sorts. Let's begin with adjustments to deal with wind.

There really are days when the air is still and hatching insects drift forever on the stream's smooth surface, and you can cast a 4-weight line without a care. But there are other days when a gale blows and your eyes water and your hat blows off and hatching flies are immediately swept away and the surface is ruffled into miniature whitecaps and your lines does everything but what you want it to do. What then?

Well, for one thing, you can look to your equipment. These are the times when you can regard an extravagant collection of rods without guilt. Set aside the split-cane 4-weight and bring out the graphite 7, for the heavier the line—and the stiffer the rod—the easier it is to cast into the teeth of a gale (*easier*, not easy). Stiffer rods also tend to throw tighter loops which have less wind resistance. Of course, heavier lines can cause problems with skittish trout, but the action of the wind, and its occasional sidekick, the rain, will disturb the water surface and render it more forgiving of heavier lines and heavier-handed casts. These are the times, too, when you may want to consider fishing wet flies, since wind will blow newly hatched insects away before trout can take them, and fish may decide to concentrate on nymphs and streamers. This is a generalization, but it's worth a thought when the wind comes up, and it may explain why no fish are rising.

But equipment alone will not defeat the wind. Nothing will, really, but technique can help an angler save face to some extent. If you're casting into the wind, the backcast will be easier, because the wind assists the lift off the water and the launching over your head, but the forward cast is harder. The only answer is power. You have to apply more power on the forward stroke. The difficulty occurs when you let the added effort counteract the timing of the cast, for you still need to let the backcast flex the rod before you can start forward. The realization that you need more power sometimes makes you rush the cast, with the attendant unhappy results. When you're casting *with* the wind, the problem occurs on the backcast—it takes more power to lift the line off the water and straighten it out behind you. The wind will try to collapse the line before it can flex the rod, and if you allow it to happen, the cast will fail. You need extra power on the backcast. When the wind is coming from your left side, assuming that you cast right-handed, you may want to throw the cast sidearm—drop the rod from its strictly vertical plane to about a forty-five-degree angle. This keeps the line away from your body, at least. When the wind is coming from your right side, you may want to use a backhand cast. The motion is a lot like a backhand volley in tennis—a sort of reverse sidearm throw.

But wait, you might be saying, how can you execute a sidearm action when the cast should be a nine-o'clock-to-twelve-o'clock-and-back-again action? Actually, the movement of the rod is pretty much the same whether the cast is sidearm or vertical, because the real secret to casting is letting the rod load. If you cast sidearm, you're only changing the plane in which the rod travels, and you can still stop the rod in the middle of its arc so that the line pays out behind at a right angle to the rod and thereby flexes it. Granted, you won't have as much air space above the water to work with, but the mechanics of the rod are still the same, and if your timing is good, the line won't hit the surface. Many fly fishermen prefer to cast sidearm all the time, because they don't relish the thought of the line coming straight back at them as it seems to do when sailing on a strictly vertical plane. This is one of those stylistic variations, much like James Joyce's earlier complaint that his foos wouldn't moos. There's room for poetic license in fly casting, but timing—letting the rod do its work—is always the key.

Having said all this, there is no escaping the fact that strong winds make fly casting tough. Good technique helps. The well-timed application of power helps. The right equipment helps. But a stiff wind still makes most of us look pretty shabby. It's a little like losing your hair—you don't like it, and you probably do all you can to counteract it, but in the end there's not much you can do about it except enjoy the fact that you save money on shampoo. Make the best of it. I know some other platitudes, but you get the idea.

One last point on weather, at the risk of nagging—wind and rain are often twin blessings. Rain, of course, makes it difficult to see, especially as the droplets accumulate on dark glasses and the overcast skies reduce the available light. At times like these, it seems that you're fishing almost by sense of smell, and you may be tempted to remove your glasses. Don't do it, until you decide that the warmth of the local pub is suddenly irresistible. If you decide to keep fishing, keep those glasses on. You won't see as well, but when you're finished for the day, you'll still be able to see.

WEIGHT

People new to fly fishing might assume that casting a weighted fly or a fly that has some split shot attached just a few inches up the leader would be easier, since they assume that the extra weight will help the rod to flex. Casting weighted flies, they think, is roughly akin to casting a spinning rod. People then try to exert a little more muscle, in the implicit belief that they will then be able to throw the weighted lure farther or more accurately.

These are unfortunate delusions. You can certainly feel the extra weight of a split shot, but you're still casting the line, not the fly. The weight does change the way the line and rod cooperate, but the primary impact of weight is to slow down the whole process. Because the fly is weighted, it takes longer for the line to lift off the water, longer for it to travel over your head and pay out behind, and longer to come forward. Any weight on the fly or near it (such as split shot on the leader) means that you have to wait even longer than normal on the backcast. So, the keys to casting weighted flies are:

> 1. Be especially aggressive on the backcast. The weight will resist your effort, and if you don't put a little more power into the lifting motion, you may find yourself with a fly stuck in your vest, or worse.

> 2. Wait. And wait some more. Give the weighted fly and the line time to lumber back through the air in order to flex the rod. If you start the forward cast before the line is fully extended behind you, the cast will collapse and the fly will land in your hat, or worse.

When you're casting weight, remember that your normal timing is going to be wrong. Your normal timing will be too fast, because when you're casting an unweighted fly, the line and fly lift off the water easily, fly over your head and pay out behind quickly, and shoot forward effortlessly. Weight ruins this timing. So slow down. Weight means wait.

But that doesn't mean you can waste any time coming forward. The problem with weighted flies is that gravity gets into the act faster than normal. Your line and fly will start falling faster than they would otherwise, so timing is important. Wait, but don't be late. Some casting instructors strongly recommend practicing with a weighted fly on a big, unobstructed lawn in order to get the timing right.

OBSTRUCTIONS

It's clear that if you need to throw the line over your shoulder and let it pay out behind you in order to load the rod, you'll need some space. The basic cast requires as much space behind as in front. Inevitably, though, because the fly caster is concentrating on a particular target or moving upstream while he casts, he forgets about where the backcast is going—and so, to a far greater extent than any other kind of angler, the fly fisherman spends time untangling his line, fly, and often himself from branches, tree trunks, bushes, rocks, and other snags of various descriptions. One way to avoid these entanglements is to turn around and survey the scene behind—and above—you before making the cast. This quick look will save time, flies, and tippets.

Sometimes, though, there *is* no space behind. Sometimes you're backed up against a cliff or a row of trees or bushes. There may be a fish rising that can be reached only from a position where a standard backcast is impossible. That's part of a trout's perverse nature. You need not despair, for a technique called a roll cast will solve the problem. Assume that you have your back virtually against a cliff and your line in the water, your rod pointed down as though you were about to make a standard backcast.

Instead of raising the rod vigorously, as you would on a normal cast, raise it in slow motion up to the vertical, twelve-o'clock position. What happens? Instead of flexing, the rod remains rigid and the floating line comes slowly back to your feet. Here you've created the exact situation that you try to avoid on a normal cast—an unflexed rod and slack in the line. But that's okay. When the rod is vertical and the line is hanging straight down from the rod tip to your feet, you suddenly bring the rod forcefully down to the nine-o'clock position. This motion creates a loop that shoots the line out in a rolling, surflike oval. The effect is similar to the "Blacksmith" cast that we discussed earlier—the line closest to the rod tip hits the water surface first and the rest of it, all the way to the tippet and fly, follows in a rolling loop. The bottom of the loop is in contact with the water as the line unfurls. The fly hits water last. As with the blacksmith cast, the roll cast is not the most elegant way to present a fly, but it is the only way to do it when you have obstructions behind you. And it's a relatively easy cast to make.

The key to the roll cast is the slow-motion lifting of the rod tip and then a forceful downstroke when the slack has reached your feet. If you raise the rod too vigorously, you'll throw some line over your shoulder and bounce the fly off the cliff. If you're not vigorous on the downstroke, you won't create the rolling loop. Instead, you'll create an interesting tangle of line and leader at your feet.

One final point: Keep the rod angled slightly off vertical as you start the roll cast. That way the line will not gather right in front of you and will be less likely to graze your shirtfront on its way toward the target.

There are other kinds of casts that you may learn over time. They're just variations on the basics, though. And you don't even need to know what these other casts are called, much less know how to do them, in order to enjoy a day on the stream. As in most things, knowledge of the basics will see you through.

I once read a fly-fishing book by a grumpy Englishman who started a chapter on casting by stating that you cannot learn to cast from reading a book. That reminded me of the philosopher Ludwig Wittgenstein who wrote a book in order to prove that it was impossible to say anything accurately. One wonders why either of them bothered. Maybe they needed the money. But up to a point, I sort of agree with both of them. Anyone who has ever tried to explain anything to a child or spouse or lover suddenly finds himself in sympathy with Wittgenstein's ideas. Words are as slippery as rainbows, and meanings are just as elusive, sometimes. Although learning to cast is not difficult, it certainly requires holding a rod and actually doing it. Reading descriptions of casting technique is no substitute for practice. Words cannot replace the feeling of the rod flexing and the line shooting. Still, having a mental image of the basic steps in the process can help. And knowing why some casts go astray can be useful in making corrections the next time. "I think, therefore, I cast" is our motto in the early stages of our angling education. After a while, it all becomes second nature; we no longer have to think about what we're doing. No longer self-conscious, no longer a hazard to ourselves or others in the vicinity (less of a hazard, anyway), we're now even able to add a stylish touch or two of our own.

"Ho, talk save us! My foos won't moos." My sentiments exactly.

The Done Thing

"Oh, Jeeves, what do ties matter at a time like this?"
"There is never a time when ties do not matter, sir,"
said Jeeves.

—P. G. Wodehouse

O N THE WALL IN THE MAIN HALL of the Grosvenor Hotel in Stockbridge, England, hangs a picture entitled "The New Gun." It depicts the arrival of a new member of an English shooting syndicate. The other members of the syndicate are all dressed alike—tweed hats, waxed cotton jackets, green Wellington boots, and plus-twos. (We would call them knickers, but in England knickers are ladies' underwear, one more example of Shaw's observation that we are two countries separated by a common language.) The old members are all carrying side-by-side shotguns, and their dogs are well-behaved Labs and goldens. The new "gun," striding toward them with a cheery wave, is dressed rather differently—camouflage pants, camouflage shirt, and combat boots. He is wearing a baseball cap and carrying a semi-automatic shotgun which looks more like a riot gun than a sporting arm. His dog is neither Lab nor golden but a German shepherd—sort of. The new man is grinning broadly and so is the dog, and neither seems aware of the dreadful solecism their appearance and equipment represent. Insouciant, the new gun looks suspiciously American. Regardless of nationality, he is definitely *infra dig*. The other members' expressions seem to suggest the presence of a blocked drain somewhere close by.

It is appropriate that this drawing should hang where it does, for the Grosvenor Hotel is the headquarters of the Houghton Club, the venerable guardian of English fly-fishing rules, the source of certainty about how things should be done, the Greenwich Observatory of fly fishing.

It is not a criticism of our English cousins to suggest that their inevitable first response to any new situation is to establish rules for the game. Rules are the key to creating and maintaining a hierarchy. Order. Knowledge of the rules and adherence to them become the ways to separate the right sort of person from everyone else. There is the "done thing," and there are the things that are "not done." People who are unaware of the rules place themselves beyond the social pale. People who know the rules and yet violate them are almost as bad. And someone who understands how the world should work will, when confronting a new situation, ask, "What's the form?"

Fly fishing is no exception. We're not talking about laws, of course, but rules, for rules can be followed or ignored without legal penalty. (The penalties are in some ways worse, for they are social—contempt and ostracism.) Although there were occasional disagreements in the Houghton Club about what the rules should be (dry flies versus nymphs), there was never any doubt that some rules should exist and should be followed.

What do you and I care about all of this? After all, what is the impact of a few stuffy turn-of-the-century English fly fishermen who made rules to satisfy their own need to make rules and exclude people they wished to exclude?

Let's put the most charitable construction on the whole thing. Maybe they were trying to protect the fishery from mismanagement and greed. Maybe they were trying in their own way to protect the beauty of the sport. Maybe the rules were their armor against the crass venality that they knew dominated the world—the venality that manifests itself in all sorts of acquisitive behavior. Anyone who has fished their waters recently would agree that they've succeeded in saving what they cherished, for the waters still provide abundant game.

And so it seems that some rules are necessary. What's more, our own fly-fishing traditions derive in part from the mother country.

We've accepted the idea that there ought to be rules, but we've fil-
tered them through our democratic, individualistic culture and
evolved rules that are far less stringent. In most cases, our rules are
pretty sensible. But even so, there is also an unwritten code that can
be traced back to both the good instincts and the snobbery of the
Houghton Club—a code designed to maintain the tone of fly fishing, for fly fishing certainly does have a tone that differentiates it
from other angling. An ardent and dedicated fly fisherman values
that tone and wants to preserve it—even someone who in all other
areas of life is skeptical about elitism and hierarchies. I've known
fly-fishing guides who in the off-season work as cowboys and fire-
men, worry about paying for car repairs, have real and desperate
concerns about retirement and whether they will have enough to

live on when they're too old to take people fishing. Yet these same guides are honestly and rightly contemptuous of some lawyers and some investment bankers and entertainment people who make seven figures a year. They're contemptuous because of poor manners in fly fishing. And a guide's contempt has nothing to do with envy. The guides don't object to a client's wealth. They object to a client's poor behavior, lack of understanding of the form—not lack of skill, but rather a lack of manners and interest in the ambiance (though most guides wouldn't use that word) of the game.

On the other hand, I also know investment bankers and others with money who would rather have the good opinion of a cowboy guide than close a major deal. (Well, almost.) A good man values the respect of another good man. Or woman. We're not talking about money here; we're not talking about equipment or clothing or anything superficial. We're talking about class—not in the social sense, but in the sense of individual worth. Form matters. So does behavior. Not much else really does matter. Certainly, it doesn't matter where you came from, as long as you know the form.

I remember fishing at a fly-fishing ranch out West where one of the other guests was from Florida. He told all and sundry about his vast experience on the bonefish flats, and his gear, from hat to outer garments, was the sort of stuff people wear fishing in the Bahamas or the Florida Keys. There's nothing wrong with that, of course, but his incessant talk about saltwater fishing and his inability to catch a trout (for which he blamed the guide) made him begin to grate as the days passed. The guides started referring to him as "Bonefish Bob," which wouldn't have been so bad if his name had not been Mel. At the end of each day he would stand outside the cabins complaining bitterly about the incompetence of his guide who, simultaneously, was telling the other guides that this guy's casting technique was enough to make strong men weep. He could hit the riverbank and the trees and bushes, but when it came to hitting the water he was overmatched.

Bob had perfected poor form. He brayed incessantly about his experience and prowess, the many trips he had taken around the world, how much those trips had cost, the inadequacies of his guide—none of which interested anyone within the sound of his voice, though his voice reached a considerable number of people. To make matters worse, he was strolling around in Colorado wearing bonefish clothing and one of those long-billed hats with the flaps in back. He managed to get everything wrong. I admire someone who is that unselfconscious. But I was in the minority. On his last day, he managed to snag a few fish, and that evening he was happy at last. No doubt the next year he went somewhere else and talked about his experience with trout.

So, then, what is the form? It's a tough question. As Jeeves informed us at the head of this chapter, ties always matter. But how does a person know right from wrong? If you agree that there should be rules, what are they?

Fair question.

It depends. That comes down to situational ethics, I suppose, but it really does depend on the locale. The Kimbridge beat on the Test is certainly one of the best spots on the river. There is a gillie's hut where you can get in out of the rain and brew a cup of tea, if you like, and there's a wooden footbridge across the river. The bank where you fish is a lawn, literally, and just behind you are a farmhouse and barn that look as if they've been there for more than one century. Not far away are thatched cottages, and wildfowl whicker overhead and pheasants squawk in the woods. It's as civilized and comfortable as a well-cared-for pair of boots. There the rules are clear—they are tacked up on the gillie's hut: "Upstream, dry flies and nymphs only." Now if you were interested in running up a big score on the Test, you wouldn't fish this way. Unless fish happened to be rising everywhere, the easiest way to take trout would be to cast a nymph across the stream and let it sink and run downstream so it ended up under the cut banks.

Someone who was adept at this technique could take dozens of good fish, but that's not the way things are done there. And note that there is nothing inherently wrong with downstream nymphing as a technique; it is just not the way they like to fish there, and a sportsman will follow the rules and so handicap himself in the name of good manners and in recognition that the rules are in part designed to protect the limited resource.

The first thing to understand about a stream that's new to you is simply the local approach to things. How are things done there? Usually there are good reasons for the rules.

Then there is catch and release. Except at some private clubs where the waters are stocked periodically with hatchery trout whose mission is to take the first fly they see and then make an almost immediate appearance in a frying pan, most American fly fishing is grounded on the premise that releasing fish protects the native stocks. This is one of the great differences between fly fishing and bait fishing, for a trout will swallow bait, and it's virtually impossible to remove a swallowed hook without killing the fish. Bait fishing is fishing for the pot. Fly fishing, on the other hand, allows easy release under almost all circumstances, because the trout takes the fly in the jaw or lip, and though he suffers a puncture wound, he will recover easily from that annoyance and go on to fight another day. The nature of fly fishing, in other words, allows catch and release. Spin fishermen use artificial bait imitations, sometimes with double and treble hooks, and so present some of the same risks to the fish as the bait angler. But even the spin fishermen are coming around to the idea of catch and release, and if you watch the bass shows on television, you'll see them releasing their fish as a matter of course and advocating the practice to their viewers.

Barbless hooks make it that much easier to release a fish, and they do less damage to the fish's mouth; they do not materially affect your ability to hook and land a fish. So fishing barbless is considered an important aspect of proper form in many locales.

We know that some of our English cousins view catch and release the way a Tory views the Bolshevist, and they have a certain logic on their side. Because their rivers are few and each river section is privately owned, catching and releasing the limited inventory of fish will eventually make the fishing too difficult, because trout, particularly browns, do learn. After a while they will not take a fly, and so our English friends must take some of their fish out now and then to prevent them from becoming too well educated. But in the U.S., where we have an embarrassment of riches when it comes to rivers and streams, we can afford the luxury of catch and release, and in so doing protect the future of the fisheries. It is, as they say, the right thing to do.

Whenever I think about the subject of catch and release, I remember a line from Bion, a Greek poet: "Though the boys throw stones in sport, the frogs die in earnest." Catch and release doesn't require such earnestness on the part of the fish, and it allows us our sport and allows us to be hunters—to exercise the instinct that many of us find so appealing. Like many fly fishermen, though not all certainly, I am also fond of hunting, particularly for ducks and quail. But whenever I kill a duck or a bobwhite or a Gambel's, I also think of Bion, and a part of me wishes there were a way to do catch-and-release hunting. That feeling generally recedes when the birds are served that evening with pasta and something chilled, but it comes back the next time out. And I believe there are very few hunters who feel nothing for the quarry, no twinges of regret about the necessary outcome of the sport. As Ortega y Gassett once said, "One hunts not in order to kill; one kills in order to have hunted." Catch-and-release fishing allows us to hunt without the twinges. And that seems to me a good thing.

But irony raises its head here, for catch and release has to some extent unleashed an unsavory tendency in modern fly fishing: aggressive score-keeping. Make no mistake, everyone keeps score, everyone knows more or less how many fish he caught during the day. And no one likes getting skunked. There's a huge difference between no fish and one fish, a far greater difference than between one fish and two, arithmetic notwithstanding. Yes, everyone likes to have some success. Further, many anglers keep detailed logs and game books, and there's something entirely salutary in this record-keeping, because these anglers will also record the type of fly used, the water conditions, the weather, and so on, and they will go back to these records, often in the dead of winter, and try to find patterns in the data, to determine what happened and why. This sort of research and analysis has added great stores of knowledge to the angling game. But that's not the kind of counting I'm talking about. No, the advent of catch and release has allowed a competitive element to inject itself into the game, a run-up-the-score approach.

I would maintain that this is not quite the done thing. People are by nature competitive, and if five friends go on a fishing trip they'll keep score—to an extent. But the difference is that it will either be a private matter or a matter for lighthearted badinage, and no one will really take it seriously. Good anglers and good friends always rejoice when their colleagues have success. The commodities-pit trading mentality—acquisitive, competitive, obstreperous—seems out of place in fly fishing. The numbers-obsessed angler who defines success in terms of daily totals is, I think, missing the point. Certainly he is not someone most fly fishermen would want to spend time around.

This all may seem like much ado about nothing, an overreaction, but I know some fly-fishing guides who have lately become disillusioned with their profession because they've seen too many clients who come only to rack up big numbers, who approach fly fishing as though it were just another competition, whose days are spoiled if they don't have a big bag at the end, who care little about the atmosphere of the sport or are unmoved by the country they're in, who care nothing for the lore of the sport or its inherent peacefulness, and who are puzzled by Walton's dictum, "Study to be quiet." Too many blowhards have taken up fly fishing because it's considered a fashionable thing to do these days. Yes, that tendency is abroad in the land, and it is regrettable. Some might say this reaction is essentially snobbish, a matter of imposing one's own values on someone else's sport. Maybe, but I don't think so. Again, we can look to Walton for insight:

> We may say of angling as Dr. Boteler said of strawberries: "Doubtless God could have made a better berry, but

doubtless God never did." And so, if I might judge, God never did make a more calm, quiet innocent recreation than angling.

Speaking of Walton, it is fair to say that his book is difficult going. Here and there he delivers a gem, such as the lines above, but by and large the seventeenth-century prose is an arduous exercise for a modern reader, and frankly a lot of his advice is either irrelevant or useless to a fly fisher, since few of us have the desire to know, for example, how to skewer a live frog on a hook ("Use him lovingly"). Walton, it seems, was an eclectic angler, and did not restrict himself to the fly. Still, every right-thinking angler will try to struggle through Walton at least once, or through the good parts, anyway. The poetry is lovely and easy enough.

All of which is by way of saying that fly fishing has a rich body of literature surrounding it, much of it having to do either implicitly or explicitly with the tone of the sport. We are told that the first English book on fishing, *The Treatise on Fysshynge with an Angle*, was written by a woman, Dame Juliana Berners, in the fifteenth century. There has been some suggestion that maybe she really did not write the *Treatise*, but people have been saying that sort of thing about Shakespeare for years, and most of us don't take that seriously, either. No, most of us, I think, would rather picture Dame Juliana sitting in her nun's habit alongside a chalk stream studying the mayfly hatch and the evening rise, figuring tactics and making notes, and then, at the sound of the bells, strolling back to the priory for vespers, lost in contemplation about the cycles of nature and the wondrous ways God had arranged them. If only she could have spelled.

That same sort of spirit informs my favorite fly-fishing book, *Where the Bright Waters Meet*. It was written by a turn-of-the-century English opera singer name Harry Plunket-Greene. Plunket-Greene fished the Bourne, a small tributary of the River Test, and their juncture is the place where the bright waters meet. There is an element of sadness about Plunket-Greene's book, because over the years he and his club mates managed to ruin the Bourne through an excess of good intentions. They overstocked the little stream and strained its natural resources, with the result that all the fish suffered and gradually starved. Further, the strain of fish they introduced was genetically inferior to the natives, but numerically superior. Like the Huns overrunning Rome, the barbarian trout gradually killed off or drove out the natives. In addition, there was a problem with pollution. Some local politician with an eye to continuing improvements decided that the little gravel road next to the stream should be paved, and the tar seeped into the Bourne, covering the streambed and spawning areas and killing off all and sundry, insects and shrimp and fish alike. It seems that our age has no monopoly on maladroit good intentions. Branch Rickey once said that luck was the residue of design. Maybe so, but pollution is quite often the residue of progress, and there are more kinds of pollution than just chemical.

The last paragraph of Plunket-Greene's book contains traces of his regret but also his feeling for the sport, and it is in some ways as good a description of the tone of the game as I have come across:

> But somewhere deep down I have a dim hope that the fairy godmother will walk along the tarry road and stop on the bridge and listen, and send a message to me in the dark; and that when the mists begin to lift and the poplars to shiver and the cock pheasants to crow in the beech woods, the little Bourne will wake and open her eyes and find in her bosom again the exiles that she thought were gone for good—the silver trout, and the golden gravel, and the shrimp and the duns—and smell the dust of the road, and see the sun once more, and the red and white cows in the grass, and the yellow buttercups in the meadow and the blue smoke of the cottages against the black elms of the Andover hill—and me, too, perhaps, kneeling beside her as of old and watching the little iron blue, happy, laughing, come bobbing down to

me under the trees below Beehive Bridge on the Whitchurch Road.

On the other hand, maybe that's a little too much. In this cynical age most people would sniff at the idea of a fairy godmother, even as a literary device. The Godfather we understand; the fairy godmother we deem unlikely. Not everyone takes such a pastoral, contemplative approach to trout fishing. Ernest Hemingway, I'm sure, never made a reference to fairy godmothers in his entire life. He was a dedicated fly fisherman all his life, except at the end when even that could not save him. But although he was avid, he was not particularly sentimental about trout fishing. Even so, he did have an idea of fishing as a form of rescue, and that theme runs throughout much of his work. In "Big Two Hearted River," Nick Adams comes home from the war and goes into the wilderness to fish and regroup. In *The Sun Also Rises*, Jake Barnes and his friend escape the dissipation of the fiesta by going into the mountains to fish. Fly fishing was always for Hemingway a method of renewal, both a symbol and an actual tonic. But he was no dry-fly snob, and in fact wrote an early article about the virtues of bait when fishing for large rainbows. Of course, in those days people generally kept all the fish of legal size, and that underscores my earlier comment about the linkage between fly fishing and catch and release—the nature of the game facilitates catch and release, whereas other methods make it difficult.

Occasional forays into the realm of bait fishing notwithstanding, Hemingway's writings on trout fishing are mainly about the use of the fly rod. And he catches the tone of the sport as well as anyone ever has in an article called "Fishing the Rhone Canal":

> Fishing slowly down the edge of the stream, avoiding
> the willow trees and the pines that run along the upper
> edge of what was once the old canal bank with your
> back cast, you drop the fly on to the water at every like
> ly looking spot. If you are lucky, sooner or later there

will be a swirl or a double swirl where the trout strikes and misses and strikes again, and then the old deathless thrill of the plunge of the rod and the irregular plunging, circling, cutting up stream and shooting into the air fight the big trout puts up, no matter what country he may be in. It is a clear stream and there is no excuse for losing him when he is once hooked, so you tire him by working him against the current and then, when he shows a flash of white belly, slide him up against the bank and snake him up with a hand on the leader.

It is good to walk to Aigle. There are horse chestnut trees along the road with their flowers that look like wax candles and the air is warm from the heat the earth absorbed from the sun. The road is white and dusty, and I thought of Napoleon's grand army, marching along it through the white dust on the way to the St. Bernard pass and Italy. Napoleon's batman may have gotten up at sun up before the camp and sneaked a trout or two out of the Rhone canal for the little corporal's breakfast. And before Napoleon, the Romans came along the valley and built this road and some Helvetian in the road gang probably used to to sneak away from the camp in the evening to try for the big one in one of the pools under the willows. In the Roman days the trout perhaps weren't as shy.

So I went along the straight white road to Aigle through the evening and wondered about the grand army and the Romans and the Huns that traveled light and fast, and yet must have had time to try the stream along towards daylight, and very soon I was in Aigle, which is a very good place to be. I have never seen the town of Aigle, it straggles up the hillside, but there is a cafe across the station that has a galloping gold horse on top, a great wisteria vine as thick through as a young tree that branches out and shades the porch with hanging bunches of purple flowers that bees go in and out of all day long and that glisten after a rain; green tables with green chairs, and seventeen percent dark beer. The beer comes foaming out in great glass mugs that hold a quart and cost forty centimes, and the barmaid smiles and asks you about your luck.

This is, in my opinion, Hemingway at the top of his game. And it reminds me of a day I spent on the South Fork of the Snake with a friend of mine, Ron Heck. We were fishing from a Mackenzie River drift boat, sliding along with the current and casting to the bank and letting the fly float under the overhanging bushes and under the cut banks where the browns and the cutthroats lie. It was easy to get a good float since the boat was, of course, traveling at the same speed as the current, and as long as you mended the line to avoid drag, you could drift the fly for a good long time. We were having good luck, for it was one of those days when the trout felt like participating, but as it got close to noon we decided to pull over and have lunch, even though the fishing had not cooled off. We didn't bother to get out of the boat, since it was only sandwiches and a drink and after that, a pipe. As we lolled against the gunwales and soaked in the sunlight and watched the fish rising all along the current line, Ron looked around as if to absorb the entire scene and said, "Now, *this* is fishing."

What's the common denominator among the views of all these people—Ron Heck, a professional fly-fishing guide without literary tendencies; Plunket-Greene, a grandfatherly English opera singer; Ernest Hemingway, the American poster boy of macho fiction? Different men, all. One answer is that the actual fishing is viewed as just one part of a mosaic, just one element in an integrated portrait; the shared idea is that consciousness of surroundings, that enhanced awareness of all the natural elements that fishing seems to stimulate, regardless of a person's style and experience. And it's not just awareness of the here and now but also of the past, for being in the country arouses thoughts of the country's past and the people who were there before. (On a cliff alongside the Colorado River just below the Glen Canyon dam, Anasazi petroglyphs were carved into the red rocks by native people centuries before Columbus sailed. Most anglers take the time to go to see those drawings, for in some way the petroglyphs enhance and clarify the day's fishing.) Like the trout that are both *in* the stream and *of* the stream, the angler is both in the scene and of the scene, an observer and a participant, integrated because of his activity—often absorbed in it—and yet simultaneously more intensely aware of his surroundings than he ever could be if he were only passing through. The fishing seems to brighten the time and to integrate the angler, so that he is no longer an out-of-place human but rather a part of the whole. Also, there is a sense of well-being that suffuses all these observations, those of Plunket-Green and Hemingway and Ron Heck. Is fishing the cause or the effect of that sense? Is it both? Most likely it is the cause. The net result seems to be an enhanced sense of place and an enhanced sense of self in that place. I would suggest that that sort of feeling is the object of fly fishing; the fish themselves are secondary. People who approach fly fishing in this way rarely make a misstep when it comes to proper form.

And of course, the other common denominator—unstated, implied—is the concern for the environment; in fact, "concern for the environment" is a shallow phrase, for the fisherman who is integrated into his sport and sees himself as part of the total landscape would no more damage his surroundings than he would spit into his hat. This hardly needs saying, and I will not dwell on it.

CLOTHES AND GEAR

> *Style is the dress of thought.*
> —Lord Chesterfield, *Letters to His Son*

Not long ago I was standing on a wooden bridge that spans the Letort, a creek in central Pennsylvania. I was staring at the water and wondering about my failures that day. Not that I was surprised by them, for the Letort is a difficult place to fish, and I never go there with any confidence. The Letort is very narrow in places. A middle-aged man in reasonable condition could probably broad-jump from one bank to the other. The water has all the characteristics of a chalk stream: smooth water, waving weeds, gravel bottom, wary trout that have been fished over unsuccessfully by countless fly fishermen. It's called a limestone creek because of the local geology—the stream rises and flows through country rich in lime-stone, so the water has the same sort of alkalinity as a chalk stream and consequently is an ideal environment for trout. On other days I had had success there, if you consider a four-inch brown trout a success. (I do, on the Letort.) But not that day. Anyway, I was standing there lost in thought when I noticed someone struggling along the bank.

He was struggling because he was encumbered by his clothing and equipment. He was a sight to gladden the heart of an Orvis dealer, for he lacked nothing. And all of his worldly fishing goods were on display—waders, of course, Gore-Tex jacket, fishing vest bulging with boxes and spools and various other items, billed hat with a flap in the back to protect his ears from errant casts (the kind of hat people wear on the bonefish flats), glasses on a cord around his neck, rod in one hand, wading staff in the other, 35 mm camera with long lens hanging from his neck, landing net strung on his back. He looked like a kid who had been dressed by his mother on a snowy school day, just two eyes peering out from inside a mound of clothing and accouterments. And everything was new. He was a human mail-order catalog. All of this on a section of the stream that you could wade across barefoot without getting the bottom of your shorts wet, a place where a one-legged man would not be bothered by the strength of the current.

I nodded to him. "Any luck?"

He shook his head. His expression suggested that he was suffer-ing from some secret sorrow, although he may have been adding up how much he had spent in order to draw a blank on the famous Letort. He offered no elaboration and trudged away, a disappoint-

ed man. I smiled the condescending smile of the veteran encoun-
tering the rookie. And it occurred to me once again that incongruity
is the essence of comedy.

This vignette raises two questions. Aside from rod and reel, just
what sort of equipment does a fly fisherman really need, and, more
fundamentally, what is the form—as regards equipment and dress?
In my mind this fellow had missed the mark, for his elaborate exterior was out of sync with conditions and threatened to expose him
to the merriment of anyone who viewed him that day.

Answering the first question is pretty simple. Here is a list (my
opinion only, of course) of the essential equipment:

◆ Waders. Neoprene waders are the best way to go.
They're flexible, which makes for easy walking,
whether in a slippery stream or on the way to and from
the car. Wading shoes with felt soles complete the lower
half of the well-dressed angler's exterior. By the way,
neoprene waders come in a variety of weights. The
heaviest are also good for sitting in freezing duck blinds,
where, although you're never warm, you can be less cold
with these heavy waders. Of course, they can be too hot
when fishing in warm weather, but then, nothing is perfect.

◆ Polarizing glasses to protect the eyes and to cut the glare
from the stream surface.

◆ Hook hone, a very handy pen-size device that is vital to
keeping hooks in good condition.

◆ Hemostat—good for removing a hook when a fish takes
the fly deeper in the mouth than usual. It's hard on flies,
though, since using a hemo tends to tear up the hackles
and bodies. It's also useful for removing cactus spines if
you happen to be fishing in the high desert country and
don't look where you're walking.

◆ Sun block and lip balm.

◆ Fly floatant.

- ◆ Clipper. A nail clipper is useful for trimming tippet material and hackles.
- ◆ Fresh tippet material and an extra leader.
- ◆ Fly box(es).
- ◆ Wading staff. If the current is strong, a sturdy stick or staff can keep you upright. Some manufacturers make folding sticks that will fit in your pocket and then snap into place when you need them. These might make more sense than an ordinary staff because you'll most likely have the collapsible staff with you in your vest or bag, whereas you'll be tempted to leave an ordinary one behind and therefore be without it when you need it.
- ◆ Hat.
- ◆ Swiss Army knife. I've heard that the difference between an officer's knife and an enlisted man's knife is the corkscrew. A Swiss officer, being a gentleman and therefore having a refined palate, will require a corkscrew for his wine. An enlisted man is expected to drink beer and therefore has no need for the corkscrew. You must make your own decision about this important question. Regardless of your choice, this type of knife often comes in handy.
- ◆ A place to carry all this stuff—vest or bag.
- ◆ Rain jacket.

A landing net is not usually necessary unless you're fishing from a boat and need the extra reach to bring in a fish. When you're wading, a net seems to be more trouble than it's worth. A fish can get tangled up in the netting, and that makes it harder to release him. The easiest way to deal with a fish is just to reel him in, tuck the rod under your arm, grab the leader, and reach down and remove the hook. That way the fish can stay in the water.

Cameras are nice to have, but the likelihood of remaining upright while wading is inversely proportional to the cost of the camera. Having a new Nikon slung around your neck virtually guarantees that you will fall in.

You'll notice that most of the essential equipment could fit easily in your shirt pockets. It is not necessary to dress up like a pack mule in order to go fly fishing.

A WORD ON SAFETY

Depending on where you're going and the degree of isolation from civilization, you may want to carry a small first-aid kit. Some people like to have snake-bite kit, too. Both items underscore the fact the there is an element of risk in some fly fishing. Wading in swift water is difficult enough, but the bottoms of certain streams can make it almost hazardous. Some streams have bottoms that consist of slippery bowling-ball-size rocks. It's no trouble at all to tumble into the water or jam your ankle between the rocks. All of this goes with the territory, but it also suggests that you'd be wise to fish with a friend when going to unfamiliar or difficult streams. Having fallen in plenty of times, and on occasion having been swept downstream for a distance, I can attest to the fact that in those situations a helping hand is very welcome. Fly fishing seems to be such a mellow and benign sport that it's easy to forget that the river and the countryside are indifferent to one's well-being. That reminds me of a line from Stephen Crane: "The man said to the Universe, 'I exist,' and the Universe replied, 'Yes, but that does not create in me a sense of obligation.'" That may not be the exact quote, but you get the idea.

Weather, too, can be a problem, which is why you want a good hat and rain jacket. And, at the risk of stating the obvious, when there is lightning, get out of the water. You make a very tempting target standing in the stream waving a graphite rod. I have seen a graphite rod that was hit by lightning, and what was left of it was the size and consistency of a cigar ash. I don't know what happened to the person holding it, but most likely he learned something.

CHAPTER 9

Only Connect

Paint should not be applied thick. It should be like the breath on the surface of a pane of glass.
—James MacNeil Whistler

Now a whole is that which has beginning, middle and end.
—Aristotle, *Poetics*

"LIKE BREATH ON THE SURFACE OF A PANE OF GLASS"—a more perfect description of the way a fly should land on the water I have never come across. And Whistler was not a fly fisherman, as far as I know. (I'm told his mother was, however; in the famous portrait she is actually thinking about the use of bait, and it is obvious from her expression that she disapproves. At least that's what I've heard.)

Now and then, despite our best intentions, the fly lands not like a breath but like a depth charge, and the shattering results send all and sundry fish down into their deepest holes. And there they stay, like submarines waiting out an attack. Sometimes that cannot be avoided. Sometimes even if one's technique is pure, the results are moist, for wind and weather play their parts. And sometimes it doesn't matter. Weighted flies are not delicate, nor are they intended to be, since their mission lies far below the surface. And, sometimes, a fly that lands with a plop or a slap will actually arouse a good fish from his musings and induce a take, especially when you are fishing a grasshopper imitation or some other terrestrial that resembles a creature that always blunders into the water using the only dive in his repertoire, the belly flop. But as a general rule, delicacy is the order of the day, especially in dry-fly fishing.

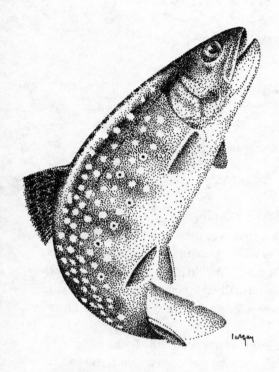

Regardless of the type of fly you use, you need to think about "presentation," that is, how you offer the fly to the fish. There are those who believe that presentation is the single most important part of fly fishing, more important even than fly design or selection. (This is an interesting but useless dispute, since it's not necessary to choose one over the others.)

"Presentation" means not only the cast, but also the subsequent action of the fly as it floats over the fish. It is not enough, in other words, to make a beautiful cast. The fly must then behave naturally; it must match the motion of the natural insects if you are to have much hope of success. You can make a perfect cast and feel the thrill of aesthetic pleasure as the fly lands like a lover's whisper, but if the fly begins to move sideways to the current the effect is spoiled, for the trout will most likely refuse it. On the other hand, you can salvage a heavy-handed cast as long as the fly is floating naturally when it arrives at the fish's feeding station. In other words, the fly could land like a brick far upstream of the fish as long as it is floating drag-free when it reaches the trout. That being true, it argues that the most important part of presentation is the behavior of the fly on (or in) the water rather than the artfulness of the cast. The cast is a means to that end, but it is not the only means. The cast is only the first stage of the presentation.

That in turn means that the presentation comes toward the end of the play, because you cannot effectively present the fly to a fish until you have surveyed the water and decided on the best method of approach. Aristotle was not a fly fisherman, though he could have been, since the earliest recorded use of the fly was in Macedonia, and Aristotle was the tutor of the most famous Macedonian of all. Maybe Alexander taught him something in return for lessons in philosophy. But even if Aristotle was not an angler, he did the rest of us a favor by stating that art has a series of stages, a beginning, middle, and end, and that a good work of art, like a good day on the river, will be one in which all three phases are well constructed and acted.

There are infinite variations in the three acts, and so maybe the best way to discuss the elements of the process, and to see it as a whole, in Aristotle's sense of the word, is to use an example, a day in which all the elements came together the way they are supposed to.

ONCE UPON A TIME ON THE HENRYS FORK...

You may have heard of the Railroad Ranch. It's a section of the Henrys Fork in eastern Idaho.

The primary source of the Henrys Fork is an enormous spring only a little way upstream from the Railroad Ranch section, which got its name because the original owners of the place made their money in the railroad business. Now it's a state park and a mecca for fly fishermen who enjoy a challenge. It's a challenge because the Railroad Ranch section has all the characteristics of a spring creek—flat water, waving weed beds alternating with gravel bottom, and wary fish who can see every move you make, because the surface is so smooth. They can even see a fly line that happens to pass through their airspace, and when they see it, they don't like it, even if it never touches the surface. Errant false casts will put them down. The trout there know that the flat surface makes it easier for airborne predators to see them, and so they take no chances. Danger comes from above, and depth is their primary protection.

You can wade across certain sections of the Ranch, if you're reasonably tall, but the current is stronger than it looks. From the bank the river looks like a long curving placid lake set down in a mountain meadow. It's the kind of water that requires light lines and long leaders and delicate presentation and patience and a philosophical attitude about defeat. I know an angler whose only success there has been one six-inch fish that he foul-hooked in the tail. And he counts it.

The first time I fished the Railroad Ranch, I went with a guide. Doug Gibson is a fifty-something fly-fishing guide who lives in the house he was born in and who knows the water around there as well as anyone ever has. If you were going to design a Western fly fishing guide, you'd end up with someone very close to Doug Gibson—lanky, a little leathery, knowledgeable, full of stories and good humor, endlessly patient with people who want to learn, not so patient with people who already know it all. He knows the country—the wildflowers, the geology, the history and, of course, the rivers and streams. He can tell you where to get a good steak or a good hat, and he's the kind of man you'd want with you if you wandered into the wrong kind of bar. Like many folk who grew up having to be versatile, having to be able to fix things, to make things happen, he projects an overall sense of competence and confidence. A good man. The first day I fished with him he observed my casting technique and ability and said, "You'll be ready for the Railroad Ranch on Thursday." I regarded this as a pretty strong compliment until I remembered that it was only Sunday. Doug figured that I would need a little tuning up before trying for the Ranch's sophisticated trout, and he was right. But Thursday did roll around, and by then I had benefited from four days of Doug's advice, and we both figured it was time to try the Ranch.

The first thing Doug did when we got to the river was sit down on the bank and take out his binoculars. While I rose to a sandwich hatch, he surveyed the surface looking for rises and, more importantly, looking for the rise of a good fish. Spotting a rising fish is really the only way to fish a big spring creek. There is no way to read the water, because the surface is smooth everywhere; there are no rocks or other natural holding areas that indicate where a fish should be. They can be anywhere. It's the same situation that gave rise to the English ethic of fishing only to a "known fish" on a chalk stream, since the best way to locate and then catch anything in that kind of water is to find a fish that is already feeding. Without those clues it's hard to know where to start. On a smaller chalk stream, of course, it is possible to stand on the bank and spot fish, and so you can throw nymphs to them even when they are not rising to take surface insects. But on the Railroad Ranch the river is too big. You need to see them rising to know where they are.

"There's one," said Doug.

The trout was holding about fifty yards upstream from where we sat, and he was only about ten feet from the bank. He was rising methodically, rhythmically. The circles he made whenever he took something from the surface were gentle. He was sipping the flies in, not slashing at them. He was picnicking, just as I was. No hurry, no urgency, no aggression.

"He's a good 'un,"—also known in guide parlance as a "hog-body-dogbody," a "pig," a "tuna," and other such terms of endearment. Oh, yes.

"Let's see what he's eating," said Doug. This is sometimes easier said than done. Sometimes when fish are rising you can examine the surface of the water and see, for example, exhausted mayfly spinners floating dejectedly down the current, and your natural assumption is that the fish are taking them. And so you tie on an imitation of that particular fly and cast away, contented in the expectation of a hook-up. And sometimes your expectations are fulfilled. But other times the fish ignore you, even though you have duplicated the insects you see floating all around you. In such cases one conclusion is that the fish are not eating the floating insects but are taking the emergers that are just below the surface, the nymphs struggling out of their shucks and trying to break through the surface tension of the water. They are close to the surface, and when the trout eats one he creates a disturbance that looks very much like a surface rise. There are people who can tell the difference between rise forms, can tell when the trout are eating emergers rather than surface insects, but when the water is smooth most of the rest of us can't tell the difference between a fish that is gently sipping surface flies and a fish taking emergers. It's especially hard when you are watching from a distance.

We waded out into the stream and spent a few minutes peering at the surface. From the bank the water looks pristine, but up close it resembles a kind of clear soup. All sorts of vegetation is floating on and under the surface. And on this day there were dozens of Mayfly spinners on the surface. They were in bad shape, but well past caring. They had expended their energy in an orgy of lovemaking and egg-laying, and now they were sprawled on the water in *dishabille*, their wings flat or cocked at strange angles, wet and disheveled, thoroughly exhausted—in fact, either dead or about to be.

"*Callibaetis*, size sixteen," observed Doug. They were grayish-white flies, and they were the only ones we could see on the surface. The logical conclusion was that the trout which was still rising languidly upstream was eating these spinners. At least it was a reasonable place to start.

Now, one of the differences between Doug Gibson and me is that he knew that these insects were *Callibaetis*. I did not. To me they were size 16 grayish-white spinners. Another difference is that Doug had some imitations in his fly box, and I did not. That is just one of the many advantages of fishing with a professional guide—because they know their water and the habits of the local fish, they carry the right flies. Tip O'Neill said that all politics is local, and while that might not be true always, it is certainly true that all fly fishing is local. Each stream, each stretch of stream, has unique characteristics, and someone who wants to do well there needs to acquire local knowledge somewhere. Many people settle for stopping at the nearest fly shop and asking a few questions. While that can be useful, it is never as useful as going to the stream with someone who really knows the water. Hiring a guide costs money, of course, but so does traveling and acquiring the equipment and paying for hotels—or camping equipment—and all the rest. Looking at it this way, the guide is one of the least expensive of your worries and the most reliable source of information that will lead to angling success. What's more, most of the guides I have met are like Doug—intelligent and dedicated people who love the game and the environment and who have encyclopedic information not just the about fishing, but also about the history and ecology of the area. If you're interested in acquiring knowledge as well as fish, a guide is the best way to go. Nor is there any suggestion that using a guide is an effete surrender to laziness. I know guides who hire guides when they go to a new stream, a new section of country. It's just the fastest way to learn the most, and learning is one of the joys of fly fishing. Or any fishing, for that matter. The cheapest way to acquire knowledge is to have a friend who knows the water and the local conditions, but friends like that are hard to come by, because most people tend to keep the really useful information to themselves. None of my friends has any local knowledge about anything worthwhile. Or so they all say.

But there's another point to be made about those *Callibaetis* spinners. While Doug knew their Latin name and I did not, I was not alone in my ignorance—the fish didn't know what those flies are called either. They *saw* what I *saw*, and if an angler took the time to observe the spinners on the water, and if his inventory of flies included one that imitated a grayish-white size 16 bug, he could catch fish. So, matching the hatch (or in this case, the spinner fall) means approximating the design (spinner), color, and size of the flies the trout are taking. You might not have the exact fly in your box, but you can try another that looks sort of like those on the water. I once caught a very fine brown trout on the South Fork of the Snake River by using a creamy mayfly imitation even though the trout was eating Yellow Sallies, which are stoneflies. The size and the color were about right, and the trout was hungry just then.

Having located our quarry, Doug and I went back to the river-bank to rig up the rod. Now in this situation a 4- or 5-weight would be about right. You need a light line in this flat water, because it is harder to control the splash of a heavy line, and any sort of distur-bance could put the fish down. A longer rod was appropriate in this case, because I would be wading at least up to my waist, and a longer rod would help to avoid turtle-snapping backcasts. A nine-foot 4-weight would be my ideal choice, but I didn't have one, so I opted for an eight-and-a-half-foot 5-weight. To this we added a twelve-foot 6X leader; here again the object was to keep the line away from the fish's field of vision. The relative delicacy of the leader was also necessary because of the nature of the water. We then tied on the size 16 Callibaetis, de-barbed the hook and added some floatant to the fly, and pronounced ourselves ready.

"Now when you wade out there," said Doug, "go slowly. Don't be making a bow wave like some supertanker, because he'll see it. Creep along like you're coming home late to a cranky baby and a wife who's a light sleeper." Well, I had experience there, so I did as I was told. "Circle around and get yourself out toward the middle of the stream, so you can cast back toward the bank to him." Approaching him from the side was necessary because if I tried to cast to him from the bank, the trout would probably see me, since the bank was elevated and there wasn't any cover to hide behind while I cast. Being in the water lowered my profile, and if I stood far enough away I would be outside the trout's window, even allowing for the light refraction that expands a trout's field of vision. I could have tried approaching him from directly down-stream, but that posed the risk of "lining" him, that is, of spooking him with the fly line, since in order to get the fly well upstream of him even with a long leader, there was the chance that I would drop the fly line just over his head. It was safer to cast to him from the side. That way the long leader would keep the fly line outside his field of vision both while it was in the air and on the water.

When I got into position I shook out some line and threw a couple of false casts far upstream of the fish, just to measure the line. Then, when I figured I was ready, I threw the first cast about fifteen feet upstream of where the trout was still rising, so that it would float down into his window.

"Mend it," came a voice from the bank . (Doug had settled down to watch the encounter.) I was expecting this. "Mend it," is a guide's second-favorite phrase after "I believe I'll have another one." As already mentioned, mending is a technique of throwing slack into the line once it's on the water. The idea is to avoid the drag that occurs when a tight line is thrown across the current; the current immediately seizes the line and pulls it downstream, which in turn, pulls or drags the fly sideways. A trout knows that real insects float with the current and not sideways to it, and so they tend to ignore anything that drags. And drag is especially damaging on the smooth surface of a spring creek-type stream, because trout get such a good look at the flies floating through their feeding stations. On a freestone stream the action of the surface might blur their view somewhat, and they might actually think that a dragging mayfly imitation is a caddis that is skittering away, and so they might strike. But that is not likely on a spring creek; the view is too good.

Mending is not all that difficult—once the line is on the water you release it from your left hand and then flick the rod upstream. This action will throw a little loop of slack in the direction of the current, so that the line floating on the surface now looks like a question mark. The belly of the line is upstream, above the fly. The current then seizes this slack, and gradually straightens and then bellies the line downstream of the fly, but during this process the fly does not drag. It continues to float in the current just as a natural insect would. Meanwhile, you use your left hand to strip in any unnecessary slack that is created as the fly line travels downstream. In other words, you leave enough slack to prevent dragging the fly, but you don't want too much, because it adds to the difficulty of setting the hook if the fish strikes. Once the belly of the line is downstream of the fly, the fly will start to drag, but by this time, if all goes well, the fly will have passed over the fish's feeding station, and he will either have taken it or at least assumed that it was just another natural that was floating by in the current. Then you can pick up the line and try again.

Which is what I did. For two hours.

It didn't seem that long, though, because every now and then the trout I was working on would stop rising. He didn't bolt or sound like a harpooned whale or do anything to indicate that he'd been spooked. He just stopped eating. During those lulls in the action, I turned about-face and tried for another fish that was feeding behind me in the middle of the river. He didn't take it either, even though my casts were reasonably competent and the floats were good.

"He's at it again," said Doug. The quarry fish had started rising again, so I turned around and tried again. Another cast, another mend, another good float. And this time he took it.

"All right!"

As soon as he hit the fly I raised the rod tip to set the hook. I had my right index finger over the line, pressing it against the rod grip, so that when I lifted the rod tip my line came tight and the hook penetrated the fish's jaw. Then I lifted the right finger so that the line could run free. Otherwise the trout would have broken the light tippet with just a shake of the head. The fish took off downstream, mad as a wet cat, and the slack that I had in my left hand ran between my left finger and thumb. I held the line lightly to avoid getting the slack tangled up as the fish ran off, and in a second or so all the slack was gone and the fish was on the reel.

"Keep that rod tip up." There was more than a trace of excitement in Doug's voice. Good guides get as much pleasure from their client's success as they do from their own. Maybe more. The last thing he wanted was for me to do something wrong and lose this fish. A big fish on the Railroad Ranch is not an everyday sort of thing. I did as I was told, and when all the slack was gone from the line and the fish was off to the races, I raised the rod above my head, still vertical. Line was tearing off the reel, and the rod tip was flexing and dancing.

"Keep the rod tip up"—these are the key words at these early stages of a fight with a strong fish. (Naturally, the tip of the rod will be bending in the direction of the fish, but the butt section of the rod should be pointed straight up.) The reasoning here is similar to the reason you stop the rod at the vertical when you cast—a vertical rod creates the optimal angle for the line to flex the rod. During a fight, the flex cushions the blows that the fish is delivering with his runs and jumps and shakes of the head. The flexing protects the leader, keeps tension in the line, and puts pressure on the fish.

The fish kept going, and the reel was zinging, and at this point, for no logical reason except that I had the reel crank set for right-hand retrieve, I shifted the rod to my left hand so that I could start cranking the reel when the fish finally stopped running. Yes, I am in the tubby Prince of Wales category of reel crankers. Why, I don't know. It's like eating succotash—I wouldn't necessarily recommend it, but I do it, and I'm not the only one. A matter of taste. Anyway, in a matter of moments the fish was into the backing, and as I watched the line disappear, the fish chose that moment to jump.

It's a thrill to see a good fish jump, a thrill akin to the feeling you got when as an amateur adolescent you asked the girl to dance and she said yes. Now what do you do? Just hold on and hope for the best. The thing about jumping fish is that sometimes they jump right off the hook. And there's precious little you can do about it. If he gets off, well, score one for the fish. It will happen, now and then, but this time it didn't. The fish went up about three feet and shook his body back and forth a few times and then landed on his side in a shower of spray and kept going, still hooked.

"Don't horse him," said Doug. In guide language, this means, "Don't try to overpower him with the rod. Let him run. But keep pressure on him." It's a delicate balancing act, and there's no way to know how to do this except through experience. You have to catch fish in order to catch fish. Or maybe a better way of saying that is, you have to lose a few in order to learn how to land a few.

The fish went down to the bottom, and I could feel him shaking his head. Maybe he was trying to rub the hook out against the gravel. Then he decided to take off again and to jump again and then to go back down and shake his head some more. This went on for twenty minutes or so. Then I felt his strength ebbing just a bit, and so I made some tentative turns of the reel, and he started coming in. Sometimes at this stage the fish will make a run back in your direction, and when you feel the line go slack you have to crank like a demented coffee grinder. (You may want to strip the line in with your left hand, because that can be faster than cranking in the line with the reel. Then, if he runs again, you can manage the line with your left hand—just let it run out again between your left index finger and thumb.) When a fish is running toward you, you get the sinking feeling that maybe the fish is gone, because the line goes completely slack, dead. But you have to keep reeling or stripping in, because this is the chance to retrieve the line that the fish took on that first panicky dash. In this case he was still there, because after a few moments he decided to change directions again, and the line came taut, but there was a difference this time: he didn't have as much strength. It seemed possible to hold him, now. So we sat there in a stalemate for a minute or so, with him trying to decide whether to quit and me holding on and wishing I had checked for wind knots.

"Try and work him over into the calmer water by the bank," said Doug. A fish running downstream uses the current against you—you are fighting both the fish and the force of the current, and that puts an added strain on the leader. If you can maneuver him to calmer water, he'll have only his own strength to resist you. And that will run out sooner or later. The faster you can get him into calmer water, the faster the fight will end and the less likely the fish will exhaust himself. Too long a fight can wear a fish out—to the point that you cannot revive him.

Doug waded into the shallows while I angled the rod to the left a little to encourage the fish to leave the main current and swim over toward the bank. Gradually he came, and it seemed that the fight would soon be over, but as soon as he caught a glimpse of Doug he took off again, and there was nothing for it but to let him go. The line sped off the reel, and the damned fish took another jump. But that was it. This time he didn't have the strength to go much farther, and I was able to reel him in little by little. When the trout got over to the bank, Doug reached down with both hands and cradled him up—a twenty-two-inch rainbow with what looked to be a disgusted expression on his face. Doug removed the hook and we took a picture quickly, and then Doug put him back in the water to let him revive.

Reviving a fish requires letting water flow through his gills. The trout has just competed in an athletic event, and he is in "oxygen debt," as track athletes say. So you point his head into the current and support him and wait. Sometimes you may want to pull him gently back and forth to increase the flow of water through his gills. In time, he will revive. It usually only takes a few seconds. And then he'll simply dart away, sadder but wiser. The key is to keep him in the water as much as possible. Ideally, you would reel him in and then reach down and remove the hook (here again, barbless hooks make this a lot easier) and then let him go. That way, the fish is never out of the water, and you really don't need to handle him at all. If you do need or want to handle him (for a photo, for example), just cradle him. Don't squeeze. And at the risk of stating the obvious, remember that as long as the fish is out of the water, in effect he's drowning.

Once in a great while you will not be able to revive a fish. It spends itself and just dies. It's hard to know why this happens, exactly. Some trout are stronger and healthier than others and better able to handle physical stress. And I suspect that some just put everything they've got into a fight, and when it's over, they're used up. It doesn't happen often, but it does happen. In today's environment of catch-and-release fishing, an angler will no doubt feel sorry when he cannot revive a fish. Fly fishing seems to be such a benign sport that it sometimes surprises us when we actually kill a fish. The best course of action in these cases is to review the encounter and make sure that we did not overtire the fish, overplay him, and, if we did, then resolve not to do it the next time, and if we did not, just chalk it up to one of those things that happens. Doug told me he once cast a weighted fly to a likely spot and brained a fish that was holding there: the hook hit the fish in the head and he was finished before the rings from the falling fly had disappeared.

"What'd you do then?" I asked.

"Took him home and ate him." It was a sensible answer to a silly question. In this case, however, our fish did revive after a minute or so, and he took off from Doug's hands as though someone had just said "Fire one," whereupon Doug grinned and offered his hand and said, "Yuh done good," which is Idaho guide talk for "congratulations." At that moment I was as happy as a parson after two sherries.

SO WHAT?

"What's the point?" you may be asking. "So you caught a good fish in the Railroad Ranch, and you feel inordinately pleased with yourself. Well, fine. But why bother us with your reminiscences?"

It's a fair question.

First, I think the incident illustrates the premise of this book, which is that fly fishing is a reasonable art—reasonable because all the elements operated as they should have. The mayflies had hatched, mated, and delivered their eggs, and then had fallen to the surface like cherry blossoms, at the moment of their perfection. The river had caught them, cradling them like a center fielder gathering in the last out, and delivered them in the current to the trout who, watching the process, had seen that they were food and had risen to the surface to take them, leaving only the rings of their rises where the spinners had been. All the actors had played their parts in this constant, predictable cycle of renewal.

The angler is the artist who inserts himself into this process and through the application of knowledge and craftsmanship creates something—in this case, a well-orchestrated event. And there is an aesthetic dimension to this event, a recognizable form—Aristotle's beginning, middle, and end. The beginning is finding the fish and developing the strategy—fly selection, equipment, the method of approach. The middle is the presentation—casting and matching the motion of the natural insects. The end is hooking and landing the fish, and then letting him go.

The actual outcome, the capture of a fish, is far less important than the participation in and management of the process, the form—understanding what to do when and executing each of the phases so that they follow on each other logically, reasonably, and lead ultimately to closure. All of the elements come into play—knowledge of the water and its particular characteristics, knowledge of the insect life, knowledge of the trout's behavior and the reasons for it, knowledge of the equipment and how to use it. Each rests on the other and each phase builds reasonably to the next. If you omit something or mismanage something, then the process stops. Whistler, during his famous libel suit, was asked by the judge how much he charged for a particular painting and how long it took him to do it. He answered that he charged two hundred pounds and that it took him a couple of hours. The judge was scandalized that so princely a sum would be charged for so small an effort. And Whistler responded that the buyer was purchasing not the artist's time but rather the experience of a lifetime. Similarly, here the significance of the event is not the time invested or the outcome but rather the ability to manage all the elements to create an aesthetically well-constructed event. The beauty of this minor art form is in the interaction of all the parts. Admittedly, this a classical approach to aesthetics, for it's based on the notion that symmetry is the key to beauty, that pieces need to fit together to create a whole, whether that whole is a building or a play or a painting or an episode like the one on the Railroad Ranch.

Fly fishing is a way of creating order in a world where disorder is the rule. The second law of thermodynamics says that the natural process is one of movement from order to disorder. Entropy. And certainly a look at contemporary society tends to confirm that gloomy view. Like most good art, fly fishing is just the opposite, for it is the creation of a well-ordered event through the application of knowledge and craft. An incident like the one at the Railroad Ranch is a small drama that is satisfying in and of itself, satisfying to the point that we don't even need to keep the quarry once we have acquired him. The play's the thing, indeed.

But there's more to this notion of a beginning, middle and end, for the pleasure of fly fishing is as much mental as physical. The real beginning is anticipation. All fly fishermen are optimists at the start of the day. Like the fat boy dressing for the dance, we all believe that this may be the time when the blond goddess looks our way. Then the event itself is the middle, and there are times when we fish well and all goes according to plan. The blond goddess not only looks our way, but actually agrees to dance. And the end is the reminiscence, the time at the end of the day when we can look back with satisfaction on a well-crafted event. We danced with her and did not step on her feet, and she smiled when the music ended. And the memory of the way it all felt stays with us. Anticipation, execution and remembrance—the three acts of a well-made play, a whole.

But are we going too far with all of this talk of aesthetics and art? In a time when rock stars are called artists and football coaches are geniuses, a reasonable person might feel that the terms have been devalued. If a rap singer is an artist, what was Michelangelo? Are we guilty of the same sort of semantic inflation in calling fly fishing an art—even if we acknowledge that it is a minor art? Maybe. Does the fact that we can cast a fly to a fish and fool him into biting allow us to give ourselves airs? As Doug Gibson might say, not hardly.

And let's be honest, most of us aren't really all that accomplished as anglers. Most of us are just sort of average. But no matter. That doesn't exclude us from this club. Even if we are not always or even usually able to create the perfectly structured event, even if our technique is mediocre and our results modest, we still can participate in and benefit from the artistic activity that is the essence of fly fishing, for if nothing else it gives us the opportunity to see things more clearly; it gives us a reason to concentrate on our surroundings in ways we rarely do as we manage the normal transactions of living. And this heightened sense of awareness, this sharpened vision is the common denominator of all good artists. As Picasso said of Cezanne:

> People never concentrate enough.... The reason why Cezanne was Cezanne is that he *did* concentrate: when he was confronted with a tree he looked hard at what was there before his eyes; he looked at it as hard as a man with a gun aiming at his quarry.... Often painting is no more than that .... You have to put all your concentration into it.... Oh, if everyone could do just that.

And then later:

> A work of art must not be something that leaves a man unmoved, something that he passes by with just a casual glance. It has to make him react, feel strongly, start creating too, if only in his imagination. He must be jerked out of his torpor, seized by the throat and shaken up; he has to be made aware of the world he is living in....

Fly fishing will not give the rest of us the vision of a Cezanne. But it is certain that we will see more, and see better, with a fly rod in our hands; we will be "made aware of the world we are living in." It creates in us the desire to learn about things that we heretofore knew nothing about, and it calls us like sirens to places that we would otherwise not think of, and when we get there it sharpens our senses by stimulating our hunter's instincts and by requiring us to look hard at what we are seeing. It generally rewards knowledge and craftsmanship, but in all cases it sharpens and clarifies our vision. And that intensified ability to concentrate, to see, is both the prerequisite and the primary benefit of this lovely and reasonable art.

*W*HY DO THEY CALL THE LAST SECTION OF A BOOK an "appendix"? Because it is useless? Something to be ignored until it has to be removed and disposed of? Perhaps. This appendix contains a list of flies that I have found effective in my travels and travails. These are flies that I have some confidence in, and confidence in fly fishing is one of those mysterious ingredients that seems to be an element in success. But the fact that I have confidence in these flies should not necessarily give you confidence in them. You have to develop your own list of favorites. And, as we know by now, all fly fishing is local. A fly that is a don Juan on one stream may be a Quasimodo on another. Further, as the year passes different hatches occur on a stream. A fly that shines at the start of the season may be a failure later on. Ergo, it makes sense not only to know what works on a particular stream but also what works at that particular time on that stream. Local knowledge is critical to effective fly selection. You can get that from the fly shop on the river or from a guide or from your own observations and conversations with the local folk. And maybe the angling magazines can help with certain streams.

Clearly, then, a list of "ten best" flies is virtually useless.

Therefore, here is my list of "ten best" flies:

Muddler Minnow

Trude

Woolly Worm or Rubber Legs Nymph (the latter is also known as a Girdle Bug)

Ant

Pheasant Tail Nymph or Hare's Ear Nymph

Royal Wulff

Adams

Elk Hair Caddis

Midge Pupa

CDC Emerger

Despite my initial caveat, some of these flies will occasionally work on most rivers. (Is that sentence qualified enough?) Rivers with grassy banks, for example, will likely hold some grasshoppers, and when the sun beats down or the wind comes up and the hoppers start jumping around, a Muddler Minnow fished dry or a Trude will often be effective. Of course, someone might say: "If you are imitating grasshoppers, why not use a grasshopper pattern?" You could, as many do, of course, but in a short list of flies I would opt for the Muddler because it is a streamer and so can be fished wet to imitate a minnow or dry to imitate a hopper. The Trude has a lovely large wing that makes it easy to see in rough water, and I have caught small brookies in small streams and large rainbows and cutthroats on large rivers and even a very nice brown on the River Test with it. Truth to tell, it is my favorite. With flies, as with people, versatility is a virtue in my view.

The ant seems to be a ubiquitous creature, and trout universally seem to like them. The two nymphs mentioned will imitate a variety of different insects and will pull fish in most rivers. The Woolly Worm suggests any of many big nymphs, and, when outfitted with rubber legs, it can be irresistible to brown trout. A guide friend of mine says about browns and the Woolly Worm: "They got to have it." (But there have been days when it has failed me, so don't get too excited.) The Royal Wulff is a good attractor dry fly, no better perhaps than scores of others, but no worse, either. It can be worth trying when things are slow and you don't know what the trout are feeding on. The Adams is an all-purpose dry fly that imitates nothing in particular but resembles a number of different mayfly duns. An Elk Hair Caddis is a very good dry fly—the buoyant elk hairs allow it to float well, and it is highly visible and therefore a pleasure to use. A Midge Pupa (there are many varieties) can be very useful, particularly when fished as a dropper; that is, as a second fly that sinks about six inches below a dry fly. Fishing two flies obviously improves your odds—of catching fish and of getting tangled. The CDC Emerger (this, too, comes in many styles) usually uses the silky feathers that come from around a duck's oil gland. (CDC means "*cul de canard*"; i.e., rear end of duck.) Whether you use this version or another form of emerger, you will need something that imitates flies coming to the surface. An alternative is to trim the wings on a dry fly so that they look like they are just emerging from the nymphal shuck.

In short, despite my words of caution at the beginning of this appendix, these flies in several sizes would make a good starter kit for any angler. Of course, if you asked ten different anglers, you would get ten different lists. Also, common sense has to apply here. The Elk Hair Caddis, for example, is a good fly on a stream which has caddis flies. But there are trout streams where there are few caddis, and therefore the Elk Hair would only be a curiosity. It might attract a fish but it wouldn't fool him into thinking it was food he recognized. Once again, local knowledge is the key.